POWER
INTERVIEWS

POWER
INTERVIEWS
Job-Winning Tactics
from Fortune 500 Recruiters

Neil Yeager
Lee Hough

WILEY

John Wiley & Sons, Inc.
New York • Chichester • Brisbane • Toronto • Singapore

Copyright © 1990 by Neil Yeager and Lee Hough
Published by John Wiley & Sons, Inc.

Library of Congress Cataloging-in-Publication Data

Yeager, Neil M.
    Power interviews : job-winning tactics from Fortune 500 recruiters
    Neil Yeager and Lee Hough.
      p. cm.
    Includes bibliographical references.
    ISBN 0-471-52117-5   ISBN 0-471-52114-0 (pbk.)
    1. Employment interviewing.   I. Hough, Lee. II. Title.
HF5549.5.I6Y43   1990
650.1′4—dc20   89-48991
                                       CIP

Printed in the United States of America

10 9 8 7 6 5

Preface

As the career marketplace becomes more complex, the demands on job seekers continue to change. More than ever, hopeful applicants need to know as much as possible about the needs of an increasingly diverse job market. This book is specifically designed to help job applicants meet the challenges of a changing marketplace. To create an interviewing book that is as comprehensive as possible, it was necessary to approach the issue from a broad range of perspectives. We believe that by bringing together a career development specialist and an expert on organizational behavior with a former corporate recruiter and chief executive officer of a rapidly growing company we have created a unique interviewing book.

For the past nine years, Neil Yeager has been helping job seekers from all walks of life make dramatic transitions. His first book, *CareerMap*, was based on his work with career changers and included material from his extensive research on understanding organizations. Lee Hough was for fourteen years a corporate recruiter for Xerox Corporation and is presently chief executive officer of the Xsell Team—a company that produces and markets videos and software. His video, "The Inside Secrets of Interviewing," has been highly successful, and his company is in the process of expanding dramatically.

By bringing together experts from both sides of the career marketplace we believe that this book provides a unique, comprehensive guide for both the new and seasoned job applicant. In addition to providing basic information on personal presentation, answers to key questions, and tips on interviewing technique, the book offers insights into the psychological dimensions of interviewing and up-to-date information on the key concerns of corporate America.

We believe that the most successful applicants, in addition to honing their skill and expertise in whatever fields they pursue, will be the ones who are highly skilled in interviewing. *Power Interviews* provides the state-of-the-art of interviewing for the 1990s. We hope you choose to use it to reach your full potential.

Amherst, Massachusetts   Neil Yeager
Scottsdale, Arizona   Lee Hough

Acknowledgments

I would like to thank my wife, Cletha Roney, for her support, confidence, and patience. I am also grateful to Miriam Williford for her continued encouragement of my writing and concern for my career. My thanks to Judy Wardlaw for her reading and feedback and to Debbie Lyon, Ellen Heffernan, and Laura Howard for their technical and personal support. I would like to express my appreciaton to my editors at John Wiley—Katherine Schowalter for her matchmaking and insight and Steve Ross for his responsiveness. My thanks also to my agent, Elizabeth Frost Knappman, for her diligence and business sense.

Neil Yeager

To Carol, you are the best.

To Neil, a good combination.

To Katherine, thanks for the opportunity.

Lee Hough

Contents

Introduction

If you've been in the job market or if you're just entering it, you probably know that career mobility is the model for the 1990s. People change jobs, organizations, and even professions more frequently than ever before. Although this increased mobility creates potential problems, it also offers great opportunities. To take advantage of the best opportunities, those seeking them must become adept at job interviewing. The need to become highly proficient in the interview process is highlighted by the fact that you will most likely engage in it more frequently than you might expect, or wish, and will face increased competition. The continued trend of mergers, buyouts, and acquisitions, a trend that most experts contend will continue through the 1990s, leaves even those who feel most secure with the possibility of finding themselves suddenly in the job market. Continued efforts at reorganization even within companies that remain intact increases the likelihood that you may no longer be needed or that you won't like the plans your organization creates for you.

Your ability to create a winning interview, to win over your interviewer, will determine the extent to which you will find the career marketplace full of opportunities or full of disappointment. Regardless of your qualifications for a position, if you cannot give a winning performance in the interview you will probably not get the job. Like any other discipline or area of expertise, interviewing is a skill, which if studied and practiced can become an important part of your repertoire of competencies.

This book will teach you to master the art and science of interviewing. You will be taught the inside secrets of interviewing in the corporate world. You will be briefed on the key trends for the 1990s, trends on the minds of every corporate leader—and every interviewer—in the United States. You will develop strategies for reading your interviewer so that you may present yourself in a way that makes the most powerful impact. You will discover what not to do in an interview by learning from the mistakes others have made. You will find out what those in the corporate world who do the hiring are most concerned about and how to address those concerns. You will learn how and when to negotiate the best offer possible. Finally, you will learn strategies for determining whether or not you should take a particular job once you receive an offer.

At the end of each chapter you will find a self-test called the Power Prep Strategy. Each Power Prep Strategy is designed to help you get the most out of that chapter and to fine-tune your skill and knowledge base in that aspect of power interviewing.

Practice and follow the advice presented in this book and you will get far more offers than you need. Refine your interviewing skill to the point where it becomes one of your strongest areas and you will find yourself with an unlimited range of offers from which to choose.

The information presented in this book is based on many years of experience on both sides of the marketplace. To avoid cumbersome language we use the pronouns *we* and *I* as appropriate. In general "I" statements having to do with clients seeking work refer to Neil Yeager, and "I" statements having to do with recruiting refer to Lee Hough.

The Basics of Power
Interviewing

Preparation is the foundation of power interviewing. There are many ways to prepare for an interview and many areas in which to prepare. The more prepared you are, the more powerful your impact in an interview will be. While much of the basics are common sense, it seems that many people, caught in the intensity of the job search, miss some of the fine points. What follows is a reminder of what to do and not to do to keep from shooting yourself in the foot.

BE REAL

Although an interview is a performance, people sometimes think that they should put on an act. Interviewers, faced with increased turnover, are becoming more skilled at interviewing. Most can spot a phoney applicant very quickly. Being sincere and forthright, while at the same time targeting your presentation to the needs of the interviewer, is the best approach. If your acting is good enough to fool a knowledgeable interviewer, you should be on stage or in the movies. Most people are much more successful if they present an honest view of themselves that matches who they really are.

BE TOGETHER

''Being together'' means paying attention to those things you usually take for granted. Timeliness, knowing where you're going, food, rest, and dress are all part of being together.

Careful attention to these details is worth your consideration because people are often judged by such factors. It makes sense to have your act together in these areas so that you aren't eliminated before you have a chance to state your case.

Be on Time

In a world where time is of the essence (in most successful companies) lateness is tantamount to heresy. It is the kiss of death in an interview. When you're late for an interview, even with a good excuse (some say there's no such thing), you immediately place yourself at the bottom of the heap. It's important to remember that the interview process actually begins before the interview. It begins when either party decides to pursue an interview. You will be judged on your behavior as soon as the process begins, not just during the actual interview.

Know Where You Are Going

If you've ever been late for an important appointment you know how stressful that can be. If you've ever been kept waiting for an important appointment you know how annoying that can be. If you don't know where you are going, your anxiety about getting there will be high. The best thing to do is to travel the route of your destination before the day of the interview. If that's not possible, at least give yourself plenty of time to get to where you're going in case you get lost.

Get Food and Rest

It's difficult to perform well if you're tired and hungry. Although the anxiety brought on by a high-stakes interview can cause you to lose your appetite or a night's sleep, make every effort to be rested and fed before the meeting. There are enough things to focus on in the interview besides your body's need for food and rest.

Dress Properly

So much has been written about dressing for success that we need not elaborate here. What's important to remember is that you will be judged by your appearance. Know that in most successful companies people are expected to look the part. The interviewer will assume that you will look your best in the interview. If your best is not up to par with their standards you will have a difficult time convincing them that you are an eligible applicant. If you're unsure of a particular organization's dress code (they all have one), there's a simple way to find out. A few days before your interview, position yourself at the front of the building where your interview is going to take place and observe what the employees entering the building are wearing. Choose the best-dressed people you see and model your interview clothes after theirs. Organizations are concerned with finding people who fit in, and this is one way of showing that you would be a good match.

If this approach is impractical for you, simply pick up one of the more conservative business-related magazines, see what people in them are wearing, and use that as a model. Another approach—if you've got the budget—is to go to an upscale clothing store, find responsive salespersons, tell them what your needs are, and let them go to work: It's what they do for a living.

THE INSIDE SECRETS OF INTERVIEWING

In addition to the basic preparation just discussed, you can do several things throughout the interview process that will save you time and energy and ensure that you are tapping your opportunities to the fullest extent. Keep these ten points in mind and rely on them for managing the interview process.

1. Avoid Personnel Departments

In most organizations the personnel department is the most obvious place to go if you're looking for a job. The problem is that in most organizations the people in personnel are the least powerful when it comes to offering jobs (unless you're looking for a job in personnel). In most cases the job of the personnel department is to screen applicants, keeping those they deem inappropriate from the real decision makers. Your best bet is to try to talk with the people in the department in which you want to work. If you find that you must navigate your way through personnel to get to your target, remember that the people in personnel are generally "gatekeepers" in the hiring process, and your task is to convince them to let you through the gate.

2. Don't Rely on Ads

Because the most obvious source of job openings is a newspaper's classified ad section, many people mistakenly assume that it is also the richest. The fact is, many jobs never appear in the papers, and most jobs don't get filled as the result of newspaper ads. We know of one marketing manager for a large computer firm, who over a 15-year period had hired over 2,000 marketing representatives yet had never placed an ad in the newspaper. Imagine the poor soul searching for a job as a marketing rep in that company and waiting for the ad to appear in the paper.

3. Specify Your Job Requirements

The worst thing you can do in presenting yourself to a prospective employer is to suggest that you're a generalist, capable of doing a broad range of jobs. Although you want eventually to convey the fact that you do have a range of skills to offer, you initially want to present your specialty. Failure to indicate a specific set of skills, those that are your strongest, implies that you're not really good at anything. The more specific you can be in identifying the kind of work you want the better. If you can do some research ahead of time to determine what areas are in demand in that company and can target one of those as your specialty, you'll have a great edge over the competition.

4. Have a Professionally Printed Résumé

This may seem obvious to you, but it is amazing how many people think that the way their paperwork looks is relatively unimportant. Keep in mind that your résumé is often the first thing someone sees that has anything to do with you. These days, when even junk mail has a high-quality look, it's important to make sure that your paperwork is top-notch. Most interviewers make the assumption that the quality of your résumé is a reflection of the quality of the work you do. If it's not top quality you're not a top candidate.

5. Tell Everyone You're in the Market

If you're just getting out of school you want to tell everyone you know that you're looking for work. The more specific you can be about the kind of work you want, the better. Saying, "I want a job in the accounting department of a large corporation" is much better than saying, "I need a job." Since you don't yet have a network of past employers and colleagues, you need to tap the network you do have. Sources for referrals and contacts include family, church members, other recent graduates, fraternities, sororities, service clubs, professors, insurance agents, brokers, and any other people you or your family have done business with. If you've already been in the work force you can use all these sources plus any others you've generated in the course of your working life. Some people have a problem with the idea of broadcasting their need or desire for new work. Those dissatisfied with their jobs often feel that they should keep their dissatisfaction a secret to avoid problems or awkwardness at their current job. Unfortunately this strategy is a great drawback to getting and winning interviews. If people who have the power to hire don't know you're looking, chances are slim that they will approach you for an interview. You need to broadcast your desires as often and as widely as possible to ensure that you get the opportunity to sell yourself to desirable buyers. This may create temporary discomfort while you're still on the job and in transition, but it will ultimately lead to many more, and much better, offers.

6. Conduct Prospecting Interviews

Sitting around waiting for a response to your letters and résumés is like staying at home, watching TV, and waiting to meet "the right person." It simply won't happen. To increase the likelihood of getting job interviews, you must get out there and interview people in your preferred arena to find out what their needs are and to let them know you are available. Although you may not get job offers from doing this (although you may), you will probably get offers for job interviews, which will ultimately lead to job offers.

A good idea before approaching someone in your field of interest, or an organization you want to work in, is to do some research on that field or company. Here's one approach that seems to work well for many people.

Contact the local branch of a national brokerage firm and ask to speak to a broker. Chances are you'll be given someone who is trying to build a clientele and is eager to help you. Tell this person you are not interested in investing at the moment but would like to start a professional relationship with an investment broker. If the broker agrees to work with you (most will), ask for any research materials the firm has on your particular area of interest or industry. The broker can get you general and specific research on a breakdown of all major firms in your industry; opinion on the industry, both short- and long-term; and information on a specific company that will include financial data, business developments, and both positive and negative events affecting the company. You will also get names, addresses, and telephone numbers that will enable you to contact these companies.

Once you have this information, approach people in the industries or organizations you're interested in. Tell them you want 15 minutes of their time to talk with them about prospects in their field. Most people will give you the 15 minutes and more. Ask them what they like about what they do, what they don't like about it, how they got started, and what they would do to break into the field today. Be careful not to take more than the 15 minutes you asked for. At the end of that time tell them you're enjoying talking with them but that you don't want to take any more of their time than agreed upon. They will greatly appreciate this consideration, may even give you more time, and will feel they've been dealing with a person who respects them.

The result of this effort will be contacts, leads, interviews, and perhaps even job offers.

7. Follow Up

The people who get the important interviews, and the important jobs, are the ones who understand the importance of follow-up. If you're talking to the right people, they are most likely very busy people. Chances are, unless you are someone they really need at the moment, they are not going to keep you in the forefront of their minds. One thing you can do to ensure that they remember who you are when they do need someone like you is to be thorough in your follow-up activity. This means sending thank-you letters to everyone you speak with; making follow-up phone calls periodically to see if their needs have changed; and maintaining open lines of communication with them, either through the mail or, if possible, through mutual network connections. When considering whether follow-up is important, think of the following reasons for doing it:

- It informs the company that you are serious about the position.
- Nine out of ten candidates don't follow up.
- It shows you are a thorough person.
- If you are not hired and the position becomes available once again, your name will be fresh in their minds.
- It allows you another opportunity to include information you may have forgotten in the interview.
- It gives you the opportunity to reiterate any crucial points.

8. Monitor Your Activities

If you're conducting a thorough job search, you're very busy. Don't rely on your memory for keeping you on your toes. If you're doing a good job seeking work, you'll probably be on an emotional roller coaster of hope and disappointment from close calls. Your focus on the near miss is important, but once that episode is over it's important to regroup and focus on other prospects. If you've got a good system for monitoring your activities, you won't be left high and dry when your dream job falls through. Keep a close record of all your activities throughout your job search and you'll be assured of an endless supply of tasks to perform that will help you ultimately to achieve your goal.

9. Ask a Friend for Help

The job search can be a terribly lonely and frustrating process. A good friend with a good ear, and most important, a clear perspective, can help you stay focused, motivated, and organized. While in the throes of this process, it is quite easy to become demoralized. Having someone to debrief you after a bungled interview (they happen to everyone) can save you much time and wasted energy brooding over what you "should have done." Having someone who is invested in helping you make it through the process, and not necessarily invested in the outcome, is what you want. Your spouse or current interest can be supportive but is probably too closely involved to be of real concrete help. You want to have someone around who's good at getting you back on track and helping you stay there.

10. Practice Interviewing

You will, we hope, never get so experienced at interviewing that you become an expert. If you're like most people, interviewing is something that you hope to do as infrequently as possible. Ideally you will find a job and an organization to satisfy your needs for an extended period of time. However, be assured that unless you are about to retire (and even then) odds are you are not done interviewing. Because interviewing is something that on the best of terms is required infrequently, it is unrealistic to think you can just do it, and perform well on command. You need to practice. You can practice by yourself in the mirror, with a friend, while driving in your car, or in your idle moments. The important thing is to focus on those aspects of interviewing that make you uncomfortable and work on them until they feel less threatening. One good strategy before a particular interview is to think of the questions that might be asked that make you the most nervous. Write them down and have someone ask you them. Keep practicing until you've formulated the best responses to each of the difficult questions. You will enter the interview far more prepared, and far less anxious. The results will be far more powerful.

LEARNING ABOUT THE EMPLOYER

In addition to preparing your personal strategy for your own performance in the interview, you need to have some information about the company you're approaching. Anyone going into an interview without having done his or her homework is at a distinct disadvantage from the beginning and will remain in that position throughout the selection process.

If the company you're approaching is publicly held, chances are their stock is traded on a major exchange like the New York Stock Exchange or the Over the Counter Exchange. These companies are required by law to publish and make available at no cost their annual and financial disclosure reports. These reports are an excellent source of information and will help you during the interview. Within these reports you will find the following:

- Information about the principals will reveal their goals and ambitions for the company. In most successful companies you will find that the values of the leaders have "trickled down" into the management ranks, thus giving you valuable information about the person sitting across from you.
- Their business philosophy will tell you about their priorities, strategies, and managerial approach. This information will begin to tell you whether you're pursuing a

company that is a good match for you in terms of your own priorities and way of operating.

- Their area of expertise will also tell you whether they are a good match in terms of both your competencies and your interests. Whereas most organizations deal with a range of products or services, they also tend to have specialities. It makes sense to target organizations whose primary areas are also your primary ones in terms of skills and interests.
- Their accomplishments will tell you how successful they are at excelling in their area and will give you an idea of the opportunities that may present themselves if you were to join them.
- Their setbacks will tell you what their weaknesses are and potential areas for problems in the future. In addition this information may suggest ways in which you might make a unique contribution, particularly if you have some strengths in areas that have presented problems for them in the past.
- The stability of their financial base is important information in terms of the organization's short-term future. A company on shaky ground may be a target of a takeover and may not be a good career risk. Many people have found themselves victims of a brief tenure because the company was bought out soon after they joined.
- What their current priorities are will tell you what they are likely to be focusing on in the near future. If their priorities excite you, you'll want to let that be known in the interview. If they don't excite you, you may want to look elsewhere.
- What long-term contracts the company has secured will tell you the long-range outlook for the organization. If you're looking for stability, the more long-term commitments the organization you're approaching has, the better.

If the company is privately held it is not under as much scrutiny and is not required by law to share as much information as a public company. Consequently information that's readily available about a public company may be a little harder to come by when dealing with a private company. However, gaining information is just as important to the interview and to your decision, should you be faced with one, about joining the organization. Privately held companies may or may not issue annual and financial reports; if not, the following sources can help you get the information you need:

- The Better Business Bureau will probably have a listing for the company if it's privately held. The bureau can tell you if there have been any problems with its performance in relation to other companies or with consumers.
- The competition is one of the parties with the most vested interest in your prospective organization. Chances are that if they are at all concerned with maintaining their market share, your company's competitiors are keenly aware of your target's strengths and weaknesses. Although this information must be pursued diplomatically, it is actually quite easy to gain information through this channel. An interesting side benefit may well be the discovery of another potential employer.
- The chamber of commerce is perhaps the organization most committed to the concept of networking. In fact, for many chambers, networking is one of the primary functions. Talking to someone in the chamber will shed a great deal of light on your prospective company, and may also lead to some valuable introductions. People who represent their companies through the chamber make it their business to promote their company. While you may have to sort the substantive from the propaganda, you can get a great deal from tapping this resource. Keep in mind that there are two sorts of chamber contacts, those who represent the chamber as an organization and those who represent individual companies. The former are good for information about particular companies and the general market in their area, and the latter for contacts and introductions.
- Current employees are the best source of information about the inner workings of a company. No one knows better what working in a place is like than someone who currently works there. Approaching people in your pro-

spective company can be well worth the effort. If you're approaching a large company, you may want to be inconspicuous and start by talking with people somewhat removed from your potential work site. If you're approaching a smaller organization, you may have to be more careful and ask for confidentiality. Getting introduced to someone who's known for discretion is best if possible. In any event, spending time with people who work where you want to work can help you get a better feel for the place and help you gauge your performance once you get an actual interview.

- Type and style of advertising can tell you a great deal about a prospective employer. Paying attention to the ways in which the company promotes its services and products will give you a feel for its marketing approach and priorities. In general the slicker the advertising, the more concerned the company is with image and the image it wants its employees to project. Paying attention to the types and amount of advertising your targeted company is doing can tell you how well it's doing, what the market is, what value it sees in its products, and what it would like the public to think about who it is.

STRESS AND THE INTERVIEW

Depending on the type of organization you're approaching and the type of person the interviewer is, you will encounter varying degrees of stress in the interview process.

Although stress interviews for the most part have gone the way of the buggy whip, stress questions are still fairly common. Less common, but reported occasionally, are stress situations, situations created to see how the applicant responds to a set of difficult circumstances.

For example, there's a classic interviewing film made by the army. In it the interviewee enters the interviewer's office and takes a seat. Shortly thereafter the interviewer asks the interviewee if he wouldn't mind opening the window. The interviewee begins struggling with a window that is hopelessly nailed shut. The interviewee is then assessed on how he responded, and assumptions are made on how he would respond on the job.

The stated purpose of the film is to show interviewers how to assess an applicant's "stress performance." Most interviewers today would agree that this artificial exercise tells little about how a person would respond on the job. Although the classic stress situation is rarely used today, a variation of it exists in what's often referred to as an "assessment interview." In an assessment interview an applicant might be given a situation to manage comparable to one that might come up at work. Typically, assessment situations, like the old-fashioned stress situation, are a little more stressful than "real life" situations.

The important thing to remember when facing stress in an interview, whether it be questions that seem impossible to answer or situations that seem overly difficult to solve, is that your stress performance is what counts. How you respond to stress questions or stressful situations is more important than the response you give or the solution you come up with.

Remember, when you start to feel increasingly stressed, what counts is not that you put out the fire but that you show you can stand the heat.

Interview Performance Anxiety

Performance anxiety comes in two forms: preperformance and midstream. It has to do with a sense of nervousness that overcomes a person either before or during an activity. Actors call it stage fright. In its preperformance form, people feel a sense of panic that they can no longer produce what they've prepared for. Actors forgetting their lines, not remembering entry points, fearing they lack the talent necessary to succeed are all examples of preperformance anxiety. Midstream performance anxiety has to do with the loss of confidence and ability in the middle of an activity. A tennis player who double-faults on a serve and then proceeds to lose a series of games, a runner who stumbles and fails to regain momentum, a quarterback who gets sacked early in a game and subsequently fails to complete any passes, all are examples of midstream performance anxiety.

Preperformance anxiety can occur just prior to an interview and can be a debilitating factor. For example, a bad day at work the day before an interview can trigger a lack of self-confidence and result in poor performance the next day. An unresolved argument at home the night before an interview can have the same effect. Even wearing clothes that feel uncomfortable or don't fit well can create preperformance anxiety.

During an interview, midstream performance anxiety can be triggered in many ways. Being asked an unanticipated question can produce anxiety. Reading the interviewer's nonverbal behavior in a negative way can create problems. Distractions such as phone calls and interruptions in the flow of conversation can throw the interviewee into a panic.

When confronted with performance anxiety before an interview the important thing is to resolve or get rid of whatever it is that is causing the anxiety. Changing your clothes, resolving conflicts, cleaning up messes on the job before leaving can all reduce your anxiety and improve your performance.

When confronted with performance anxiety in the course of an interview the important thing is to recognize it early, overcome it, and regain composure. For example, some actors' strategy for overcoming stage fright resulting from the size or makeup of an audience is to find one person in the crowd who looks friendly and inviting and play to that person—as though he or she were the only person in the audience. This would be a good strategy to remember for a group interview—a frequent cause of performance anxiety. Identify the one person in the room who seems most receptive and least threatening and play to that person.

One common mistake that often triggers interview performance anxiety is the perception on the part of the applicant that whatever happens in the room is directly related to the interview. Applicants read all sorts of things into the interviewer's behavior that can cause an anxiety reaction. Remember that interviewers have a lot on their minds other than your performance. As long as you're presenting yourself in the best light possible, chances are good you will make a positive impression. Sometimes remembering not to worry can be the best remedy to interview performance anxiety.

One strategy many athletes use to overcome midstream performance anxiety is to visualize themselves succeeding in the very act in which they just fumbled. The quarterback might envision himself throwing a touchdown pass, the runner tearing through the ribbon at the finish line, the tennis player taking the set. One thing you might try in an interview in which you are fumbling is to imagine yourself receiving the offer, or better yet, arriving for your first day on the job.

Whatever approach you take, be aware of the possibility of performance anxiety affecting you both before and during an interview. Interviews are nerve-racking experiences by design. You don't need the burden of performance anxiety to tax you further. Do what you need to do to avoid and shed performance anxiety and you will undoubtedly do better in the interview—and get more offers.

WHEN THEY JUST SAY NO

A recent skit on "The Tracy Ullman Show" vividly illustrates the way the interview process works—and why the best candidate doesn't always get the job. The skit takes place in a corporate conference room. Three applicants (a man and two women) have just been told that they are equally qualified for a position. For a final decision each candidate is asked by the woman interviewing them to do something creative for one minute with "the magic box." The magic box is an old wooden filing drawer filled with a variety of items including clothespins, dental floss, a carpenter's saw, four full soda bottles, wooden dowels, bandages, and a cap gun with exploding caps.

The male applicant goes first and begins frantically rumaging through the magic box. As time is about to run out on his minute he desperately grabs two clothespins, places them on his lips, and quacks like a duck. Disappointed in his own performance, he sits down. Tracy goes next. She pins up her skirt with the two clothespins, removes the bottle caps, and pounds them into the soles of her shoes. Next she takes the exploding caps from the toy gun and places them around the top edges of the boardroom table. She then jumps on the table and does an elaborate song and dance, tapping her way over the exploding caps for accompaniment. Pleased with her performance, she sits down.

The next woman, the final candidate, walks gracefully over to the magic box, takes the dental floss, and fastens it to both ends of an 18-inch dowel. She then picks up the carpenter's saw, returns to her seat, and proceeds to play a tonally perfect rendition of "Somewhere Over the Rainbow," playing the flossed dowel against the saw as though it were a violin and bow.

At the end of the three one-minute performances, the woman making the decision bypasses the two female candidates, who clearly outperformed the man, and congratulates him on winning the job. After the two disgruntled women leave, the interviewer confronts her new charge and tells him there are two reasons he got the job. "First," she says, "you could never be a threat to my position, and second, I don't find you the least bit sexually attractive."

Aside from the humor and sexual role reversal displayed in this skit, the scenario points to a key aspect of the interview process, the notion of rejection. If you are rejected after an interview, try not to take it personally. So devastated are some people that it takes them weeks if not months to recover and begin seeking other interviews. Keep in mind that the interview process is a flawed one and that most often the reasons for your rejection have nothing to do with you or your performance. Like the characters in the Tracy Ullman skit, you are subject to variables far beyond your control. Prepare as well as you can; perform your best; take rejection as their loss, not yours; and move on to your winning interview.

HANDLING DISCRIMINATION

Another aspect of the interview process highlighted in the story of the magic box is the notion of discrimination. Regardless of who you are, you are vulnerable to discrimination. Whether it's your sex, your age, your race, or some other less overt factor, the possibility exists that you will be discriminated against in the selection process. Although there are laws to protect applicants against some forms of discrimination, the reality is that discriminatory acts are committed in interviews every day in all sorts of organizations.

Handling discrimination in an interview can be tricky. If someone asks you an illegal question that you believe is intended to discern information that could be used against you (for example, questions about your marital status, age, or ethnic background), you have several choices. You can answer the question and hope the information is not used against you. You can refuse to answer the question on the grounds that it is private information. You can point out that the question is illegal and lodge a formal complaint. You can bring suit against the interviewer, claiming discrimination.

As you can see, the responses range from the compliant to the litigious. The response you choose to take should be based on your own moral values and your desire to work in that organization. Most likely, the more confrontive you are in your response to a potentially discriminating question, the less likely you are to be asked to work in that organization. Some people, offended by a certain question but anxious to work in the organization, would respond cooperatively during an interview but would voice their disapproval at the illegal question once they are part of the organization and in a more influential position. Others decide not to pursue work in a given organization because of its discriminatory attitudes. Others feel a moral obligation to fight discrimination whenever it arises and feel compelled to fight it either through a formal complaint or legal challenge.

Handling discrimination is a very personal matter, one that does not lend itself to prescription. As a job candidate you need to be aware of its possibility and you need to be ready to respond in a way that feels most appropriate to you, given the particular circumstances, your own moral standards, and your motivation for procuring a particular job offer.

WHEN TO PULL OUT THE STOPS

While most interviews are like walking a tightrope—the goal being to get to the other end—on occasion there is call for a different metaphor. If you're applying for a job for which the competition is wide open, you need to put in a steady, careful performance. However, occasionally you'll find yourself in the position of being part of a pool of interviewees for a job that is already filled. You may be wondering why busy professionals would waste their time in such a case. There are several reasons. They may be trying to present an image of fairness. They may be meeting affirmative action requirements. They may be trying to keep their inside candidate in suspense. For whatever reasons, finding yourself in an interview when the decision has already been made is unfortunate. However, there are ways to take advantage of the situation.

One man we know was applying for a job as director of finance for a medium-sized company. On his way into the interview he noticed the name of a man on the directory whose title was acting director of finance. He got a sinking feeling that the interview would be a waste of time. He assumed, accurately, that unless the acting director was a real turkey, the job was probably not really available.

During the interview he looked for signs to support his fears. After receiving several signals that the job was not really open, including several comments about what a good job the acting director was doing and a decided lack of attentiveness by the interviewer, he decided to take a risk. As he tells it, this is what he said: "It seems to me that you've got a really good inside candidate for this job, and unless I'm mistaken he's clearly the front-runner. I'm sure I could do this job well, but if I were in this other man's shoes I'd feel pretty confident. I wonder if there are any other positions in this organization that you might consider me for or suggest I go after."

Now, some of you may be thinking that this man was foolish and took a big risk. You'd be right if he had made his move on a whim. However, if his judgment told him he was in a dead-end interview, he had nothing to lose and everything to gain.

In this man's case he was channeled (or as he put it, networked his way) to another division, where he was offered a very good position.

The moral of the story: When the high wire is taken you may want to try the trapeze.

PERSISTENCE AND STAYING CLOSE TO THE INTERVIEWER

Don't get confused by what sounds like guidelines for salespeople rather than job candidates. Because interviewing is so much like sales—you are the product—we will from time to time borrow advice from the sales experts. This particular piece of advice is important to remember. You need to remind the interviewer of your interest in the job, you need to ask for the job, and you need to pursue the job until it is no longer available.

I once interviewed 20 people for an opening. After two sets of interviews the selection narrowed to two candidates. One candidate had a strong background and interviewed well, but he never asked for the job and was not overtly enthusiastic. The other candidate had less experience and was not quite as smooth in the interview. However, she was very enthusiastic and specifically asked for the job, twice. Before I made the hiring decision I replayed the interviews in my mind; my choice was to hire the positive, aggressive candidate. Her persistence was what I remember most about those interviews.

Just as the salesperson has to ask for the order, you have to ask for the job. While you want to be careful not to be obnoxious in the pursuit of a position, you want to make it clear to the interviewer that you are interested in the job and believe that you are a good match. Asking for the job in the interview and in subsequent contacts you have with the potential employer is a good idea. Remember, most people have a lot on their minds other than filling the position you want. If you ask them for it and they were leaning somewhat toward you anyway, they just might say yes.

WHO'S THE BOSS?

This may seem obvious, but we've known of more than one occasion when new employees arrived on the job to find that they'd be working for someone they never met during the interview process. This can be particularly unsettling if part of the applicant's decision to take the job was based on a presumed reporting relationship. Since the superior-subordinate relationship can be the linchpin of a good job, it is critical to make sure you know who's in charge. This information is quite easy to find out: If it's not offered in the course of the interview simply ask before making any commitment.

It is also wise to look beyond the immediate superior and find out what the chain of command is between you and the top. This can be helpful for several reasons. It can tell you at what level you'd be entering the organization, and it can also indicate how many steps up are available to you. Beyond that, it can give you clues about how valued your unit and function are to the company brass.

In general those positions considered most critical to the organization's leaders have a minimum of intermediaries between the top and the particular employee. If the chain of command between you and the chief executive officer (CEO) has a multitude of links, you're probably not too highly valued. The closer you are to the base of power, the more valued you are—and the greater the opportunities will be.

THE OTHER SIDE OF THE FENCE

An important thing to remember is that interviewers have a lot at stake in the interviewing process. Companies lose millions of dollars every year because of poor hiring decisions. Although interviewers may not have as much at stake as interviewees, their reputation, the productivity of their unit, and in some cases their jobs depend on choosing and hiring the right people for the right jobs. While different organizations approach the process in different ways, it is likely that any organization you get offers from will take you through at least two steps, the initial interview, or screening interview, and the in-depth interview. It is helpful, in order to get as full a picture of the interview process as possible, to look at the situation from the other side of the fence. After reviewing the interviewing procedures of many companies, the Xsell Team has devised the following review of the interview process from the perspective of the interviewer. Following is a review first of the objectives of the initial interview followed by a review of the steps likely to occur in any interview. This information is intended to give you a bird's-eye view of the interviewer's priorities to ensure that you meet their needs in the process.

Objectives of the Initial Interview

The interview is a means of obtaining information about a candidate in a limited time period. At its best it is a complete and succinct process of evaluation. At its worst it is an unfocused conversation that yields little helpful information. The key to successful interviewing is the interviewer's ability to focus the interview by being clear about the needs of the organization and becoming familiar with the qualifications of the candidate.

The interview is used to discover the candidate's likelihood of success by probing his or her background. A candidate's patterns of involvement; achievement; and success at work, in school, and socially are patterns that will be repeated in the business environment. This premise, that a person's potential for success can be determined by an analysis of his or her background, is the basis for the decision of whether or not the candidate should be given further consideration.

In the interview it is necessary to:

- Discover and evaluate the candidate's history in light of the corporation's predetermined requirements.
- Evaluate those elements that can be determined in a face-to-face meeting (that is, ''business presence,'' appearance, personality, and communication skills).

- Provide candidates with general information about the corporation and specific information about the job for which the candidate is interviewing

The key factors to cover are these:

- Review background of candidate.
- Evaluate patterns of success.
- Test for key traits and characteristics.
- Observe behavior during the interview.
- Make a decision to take candidate to next step or reject.

Steps in the Interview Process (from Interviewer's Perspective)

1. Review résumé (before interview).

Look for patterns of growth and outstanding accomplishments, or lack of growth and lack of accomplishments. Note items to be pursued. Also check career objectives.

2. Greet candidate and establish rapport.

Do what's necessary (within reason) to make the applicant feel welcomed and relatively relaxed.

3. Confirm candidate's interest in the corporation and explain agenda.

Explain to the candidate that he or she will be asked some questions, that information about the corporation and specific job opportunities will be presented, and finally that he or she will be given a chance to ask questions.

4. Probe for key characteristics.

The purpose of probes is to ask applicants to expand on information provided in the résumé. In addition, probes give candidates the opportunity to demonstrate verbal ability, organization, confidence, and poise. Probes should be sufficiently broad in scope to require the applicants to analyze their own thoughts and expand on personal experience; for example, "Tell me more about your role in this project." Remember, there is little value in simply rehashing information provided in the candidate's résumé.

5. Provide a brief overview of the corporation.

- Discuss in general how the applicant's experience and academic training might fit into the organization, including possible career paths and work locations. Be careful, however, not to create unrealistic expectations.
- Describe the corporation from your perspective by pointing out how specific policies, benefits, and philosophies have affected your career.
- Stress what is unique about this corporation rather than what is common to most business organizations.

6. Solicit questions.

Use this time to clear up questions the candidate has and also to substantiate your evaluation of the applicant's interest in employment with the corporation. (If the candidate has no questions about the organization or the job, suspect a lack of interest.)

7. Close the interview.

Be explicit. The candidates should be informed that their qualifications will be reviewed by various managers in light of current and/or anticipated openings. After the management review, the next step, if appropriate, may be an invitation to the corporation or a branch office for further interviews. In every case make it clear to the candidates that they will hear from the corporation within a reasonable period. Never reject applicants in an interview or leave them with the impression that they will probably receive a job offer.

8. Complete evaluation forms.

Record your impressions of the candidate immediately. You should make a decision on the candidate at that time because your perceptions of that person will never be more clear.

The preceding information reviews the steps likely to be taken by most interviewers in the screening, or initial, interview. Subsequent interviews are far less predictable and vary in scope and content. The interviewer's style, the culture of the organization, and the nature of the position will determine how subsequent interviews are held.

For example, Harvey MacKay, president of MacKay Envelopes and author of *Swim with the Sharks Without Being Eaten Alive* has a unique approach—and the lowest turnover rate in his industry. MacKay and his staff go through an elaborate selection process for everyone in the organization. It takes anywhere from two months to three years to fill key positions. What MacKay does is get to know applicants extremely well through interviews with the candidates, their families, and even their neighbors. He then spends time with the candidate, doing a variety of things including leisure activities of the applicant's choice.

While this unconventional approach may seem a bit exaggerated for some of you (although some of you no doubt would welcome the opportunity), it illustrates the many ways companies handle the selection process.

Regardless of the approach your interviewer takes, the way to have a successful in-depth interview is to prepare yourself by studying the seven key evaluation factors, the twelve trends to take you over the top, and the strategies for making the all-important connection, outlined in Chapters 2 through 5.

INTERVIEWING FOR JOBS IN SMALL BUSINESSES

The Hidden Economy

Although the diversity of interviewing is such that there is no way to predict what kind of interview you will have when approaching a particular organization, there are some predictable patterns. What has been covered in this chapter so far applies to all types of organizations, but there is a category that is so often overlooked by the job seeker that we choose to highlight it here. When searching for work most people approach the obvious organizations, the high-profile companies whose names everyone is familiar with. By doing so they are overlooking the ''hidden economy.''

The hidden economy consists of millions of smaller firms, the vast majority of which are privately held, publish little information about their activities, and rarely appear in the business press. Since 1980 the hidden economy has created more jobs in the United States than have been created in Japan and Europe. Here are a few statistics to show what job shopping in the small business market offers.

- From 1980 to 1987 the non-Fortune 500 economy created 17 million jobs. During that same time the Fortune 500 eliminated 3.1 million people from their payrolls. This is the equivalent of laying off the entire work force of Massachusetts.
- Ninety-seven percent of all the businesses in the United States have fewer than 100 employees. This represents approximately 12 million firms, whereas there are only 250,000 firms with more than 100 employees.
- Two out of three workers get their first jobs with small businesses.

The good news is that the small business market is vibrant, growing rapidly, and holds tremendous opportunity for job seekers. The bad news is that finding these jobs and preparing to interview for them is more difficult than with larger companies because of the following factors:

- Most of these companies are privately owned rather than publicly owned.
- Many of them do not publish financial information such as annual reports.

- Job descriptions in these companies are seldom well defined.
- The interview process tends to be much more informal.

The Question of Stability

Many people shy away from small businesses because they fear the instability of an organization not protected by large numbers. However, statistics show that since 1980 fewer people were laid off in small companies than in large ones. This does not mean that you have nothing to fear with the small business; you do need to be careful. When approaching a small organization you want to look into its stability by asking questions about its future and making some judgments about the chances of being fired. One of the advantages to keep in mind—the plus side of the lack of stability—is the opportunity that small businesses afford for moving up in the organization. While large organizations are reducing the ranks of their upper-level people, small organizations often look to insiders to carry more of the responsibility. Consequently, if you pick the right small business you may find yourself moving up faster than you ever could in a large organization.

Getting the Interview

Networking is even more important in this arena than in others. Tell everyone you know you are looking for work and that you want to work for a small company. Because of their informal approach small companies are often more responsive to networking. If you know someone in one of these companies ask that person to help you get an interview. Because the companies are small, most employees know the people who do the hiring and are able to get their attention. Also, it is often a feather in their cap if they help get a good candidate in the door.

Check the bulletin boards and placement offices of the community colleges in the area. Many small companies look for employees by using these sources. Check the newspaper listings more carefully for jobs in these companies. Even the part-time listings can sometimes lead to full-time positions.

Use prospecting interviews more extensively. Again, these organizations have a harder time finding good people because fewer people know about them; consequently they are more responsive to people who approach them for inquiries and/or jobs.

The Interview

You should approach an interview with small businesses by using the same strategies for power interviewing outlined in this book; however, there are a few modifications to consider.

Since you may not have as much information on these companies, you will have to get a better understanding of the company and the opportunity by asking questions. Make a list ahead of time of all the things you'd like to know about the company and the job and bring it to the interview. Small organizations don't expect you to be as well briefed on them as large ones do. Your questions should include, among others, the following:

- What is the company's history of sales, profits, and employee growth for the last three years?
- What are the company's goals and direction? That is, does it have a plan and a vision for the future?
- What would be the career path for the job you are seeking?
- Why is this job available? Is it a new position created by growth or is it available because of the promotion or termination of the person who previously held the job? A conversation with that person could be very helpful as an indicator of both the job requirements and the expectations. It could also give you a perspective on the culture of the company.

Finally, remember that smaller companies are less likely to have jobs that are very specific or that have well-defined responsibilities. They often require employees capable of a wide range of duties. The key may be your flexibility, your ability to adapt to whatever the needs are of that company. You may want to stress this feature in your interview along with your desire to learn and grow in the small company environment.

SUMMARY

This chapter covered the basics of power interviewing. Although much of what was said may seem like common sense to you, we all know how uncommon common sense really is when it comes to actual practice. Consider the advice in this chapter as a base for your performance and you're on your way to mastering the power interview.

POWER PREP STRATEGY I

What are you going to wear to the interview? _____

_____

_____

Are there any things you need that you don't have? If so, what? When are you going to get them? _____

_____

_____

Is your résumé professionally printed? If not, when and where are you going to have it done? _____

_____

_____

What do you know about this employer?

Business philosophy_____

_____

Areas of expertise_____

_____

Accomplishments_____

_____

Setbacks_____

_____

Financial stability _____

_____

Current priorities _____

_____

Long-term contracts _____

_____

If possible get answers to the preceding seven items before entering the employment interview.

What is the salary range for this position? _____

What is your desired salary for this position? _____

What is the minimum salary you would accept? _____

What benefits do you require to accept this position? _____

What "perks" would you like to receive in addition to basic benefits?

_____

How much vacation time do you want? _____

What is the minimum amount of vacation time you will accept? _____

_____

What aspects of this interview make you feel the most nervous? _____

_____

_____

_____

What can you do to get over the nervousness before the interview (for example, practice tough questions or talk with someone about your anxiety)? _____

_____

_____

_____

When will you set aside some time to do these things prior to the interview? _____

2

The Winning Profile:
The Seven Key
Evaluation Factors

If you have decided to use this book, you probably see yourself as a winner or a potential winner. You have decided to use all your personal resources, your personal power, to conduct a power interview, one that will ensure the most possible offers for the best possible jobs. By so doing you have set your sites high. To achieve your goal you need be clear about what you have to offer and what the companies you wish to work for want. You also need to know what to do to convince the people who hire in those companies that you are a good match.

Over the years we have learned a great deal about creating matches between prospective employees and the best employers. In this chapter we will outline what the people who have the hiring power consider to be the most important assets for prospective employees.

We have narrowed these assets down to seven variables, what we call the seven key evaluation factors. What follows is a discussion of the seven factors, what they look like in action, and what you can do to convince someone that you possess each of these key traits. There are many ways to show that you have the key characteristics. One of the best ways to do this is to draw from your past. Your ability to convey your use of these traits in action will greatly enhance your performance. That is, telling stories illustrating your past success in using each of these traits can be very convincing. To show how this is done for each of the categories we will present a Trigger Story. The Trigger Stories are examples of stories that have successfully convinced an interviewer that the storytellers have a particular trait. The Trigger Stories are told in the first person to demonstrate how they can actually be used.

FACTOR ONE

Aggressiveness and Enthusiasm

People who exhibit this factor are self-confident and self-assured. The way they present themselves, the language they use, the stories they tell to illustrate their success, all indicate that they are high achievers. They are people who make it clear that making a significant contribution to their organization is a top priority in their lives. They are not afraid to show their enthusiasm or their willingness to compete. Because of increased global competition and much talk about America's ''crisis in productivity,'' it is imperative for the applicant wanting to score high in this factor to demonstrate a high level of energy and a strong commitment to the goals and priorities of the company.

By choosing to pursue work in the corporate world you make a statement about your goals and priorities. While many companies are becoming increasingly aware of the needs of their employees and the importance of responding to those needs, the essential point in hiring is ''What can this person do for this company?'' The corporate recruiter is looking for someone who has drive and ambition, someone out to prove how good he or she really is. Along with the drive to excel, the successful applicant must demonstrate a genuine enthusiasm for the company's product or service. Think for a moment of a good salesperson you know, someone who's really good at selling whatever it is the person sells. One thing you've probably noticed about that person is that he or she believes, or at least seems to believe, in the product or service sold.

Since enthusiasm is a key evaluation factor, it makes sense for you to pursue work that deals with a product or service that excites you. Feigning enthusiasm is a lot harder than projecting genuine enthusiasm. You may at first think this limits your options, but it doesn't really. There are many companies from which to choose. If you're aiming high, chances are the company you've chosen became successful by producing a high-quality product or service. All you need to do is find those companies that produce and sell things you're interested in, make sure they're the best at what they do, and let your genuine enthusiasm pour out. One thing to keep in mind is that enthusiasm is contagious. I once had a student who was a regional distribution manager for a large restaurant chain. This man was so enthusiastic about the quality of food being produced at his restaurants that after listening to him talk about it a few times I found myself stopping at those restaurants more frequently and admiring their quality. The point is that his genuine expression of enthusiasm convinced me that his was a high-quality product and that he was doing an excellent job.

In addition to a sense of enthusiasm about the product or service of your target companies, you need to express a general sense of enthusiasm for work itself. If you're looking for a job that gives you the time and freedom to pursue outside interests, the corporate world is not for you. To convince those doing the hiring that you are a good match for them, you must convey a sense of determination, a willingness to ''go the extra mile'' for the company. If you're not willing to do this it will be very difficult to convince someone that you're right for the position. They probably won't hire you, and they're probably doing you a favor.

Trigger Story   One of the periods I'm most proud of from my working life was the time I first started working at InfoTech. I was hired as an assistant marketing manager to help in the development and launching of their new personal computer. After I was there about two weeks the marketing manager had a heart attack. As you can imagine, that threw the whole project into a tail spin. Management immediately started talking about pushing the project back for six months. I thought about it that night, and realized that in the fast-paced personal computer market six months would spell disaster. I decided I would do what I could to fend off the potential loss.

The next morning I went in to talk with the vice president in charge of our division. I told him that I was concerned that a six-month delay would cause irreparable damage to our product line. I also told him that I thought we had the best product out there and that given a timely release we could capture a good part of the market. He agreed and started lamenting about what a blow the marketing manager's illness was to the company (not to mention to the marketing manager).

At that point I interrupted him and told him I had a plan. I then took out the outline I had worked on the night before showing how with a little reorganizing I could pick up some of the marketing manager's responsibilities until he was able to return. I sketched out a plan that involved my dropping some of my current tasks, giving them to someone else, and picking up the key tasks of my boss. I told him there were some new things I would have to learn but that none of them seemed too overwhelming. I let him know I was willing to do whatever it took to make this work. He reluctantly agreed to make me acting marketing manager for this project. The next six months were unbelieveable. I learned a lot and worked constantly. We had a successful first season and our product eventually became a big seller.

FACTOR TWO

Communication Skills

As the world, and particularly the U.S. corporation, becomes entrenched in the information age, the importance of effective communication cannot be overstated. If information is power, then those who communicate best are the most powerful.

One aspect of the emergence of the information age is the transition of the U.S. economy to a service economy. So pervasive is this shift that one major Fortune 500 company recently announced it was shifting its emphasis from a production-based computer company to a service-based company. Since quality service depends on the ability to communicate with the customer, a prospective employee's ability to communicate becomes paramount.

Being able to communicate means being able to convey information, ideas, and attitudes in a lucid and persuasive manner. In an age where scarcely a day goes by without reports in the media on the failure of schools to produce literate graduates, effective communication skills become a highly prized commodity in the marketplace. Prospective employers want to see not only that you have basic competence in speaking and writing clearly but also that you excel in this area. Your ability to demonstrate that you have superior communication skills and that you can effectively influence others through the written and spoken word will greatly increase your chances.

You need to be prepared to demonstrate in an interview your communication skills. You will be judged by the extent to which you communicate clearly and effectively. Unless you're asked to produce a writing sample (more companies are doing this), you may be evaluated only on your oral communication skills. Here you will be examined for your ability both to convey and to process information. Your ability to demonstrate a command of the English language will take you far in the interview process. However, beyond mastery of the language, your performance in the interview should also demonstrate your ability to manage the communication process. If in the course of an interview there is an incident of faulty communication (more often than not, there is) this is an ideal opportunity to demonstrate your abilities. Don't be afraid to clarify what you've said if it was misunderstood or to ask for clarification if what you've been told or asked is unclear. Most people won't do this in an interview; however, demonstrating a commitment to and an affinity for clear communication will make you stand out from the crowd.

Trigger Story One of the most exciting experiences I've had in my work life was when I was asked to prepare and deliver a speech in front of 500 managers. I had been working for Premium Manufacturing and had gotten involved in an employee participation program. A group of us were meeting on a weekly basis to try and iron out some production problems. Because I was a vocal member of the group during the early stages I was asked to be the chair. Since I had never done this before I didn't know how to proceed. I bought a book on running meetings and had things moving pretty smoothly within a few weeks.

Eventually my group was able to make some real changes in the production process. Through our discussions we were able to cut production time by 20 percent in several areas and devised a way to reduce the number of rejected pieces by 30 percent. The plant manager was so impressed with our results that he asked me to make a presentation at a national meeting of company managers. I agreed to do it. When he told me I would be talking to a group of nearly 500 managers I thought I was going to collapse. I had never spoken in front of more than 25 people at a time.

I got a few books on public speaking and began talking with people I knew who had done some. Eventually I got more comfortable with the idea. I spent a good deal of time preparing for the presentation, writing extensive notes on cards. When the time came to speak I was pretty nervous, but well prepared. In fact, when I actually gave the speech I hardly looked at my notes at all. When I was done several people approached me and told me what a good job I had done. I've since been asked to speak at several conferences. I still get nervous, but it gets easier every time.

FACTOR THREE

Record of Success

Since most successful companies pride themselves on being the best, it makes sense to assume that they would hire only people who they believe are the best at what they do. While you may be highly trained and very capable of performing at an excellent level, unless you have a history of success you will have a difficult time gaining access to the companies you most want.

Most people interested in good corporate jobs do have respectable track records. The problem is that many people cannot explain their success. If you can define the reasons for your success, you can transfer these traits to the skills and characteristics necessary for the job you want. When you discuss your success be sure to delineate your role in the activity. For example, if you chaired a successful fund-raising campaign, state how your presence made a difference and was an integral part of the project's success. The key here is being able to translate previous successes into terms that get and keep the attention of your interviewer. If your past successes are similar to the kinds of challenges likely to come your way in your desired job, speak freely about them in the interview. If your past successes differ from anticipated challenges (for example in the case of a career change or a new graduate) don't despair; just be ready to describe the relevance of past successes to the work ahead.

The important thing in conveying a record of success is to present yourself in a way that highlights your uniqueness. Too many people resort to hackneyed expressions that sound all too familiar to the interviewer. It's important here to remember that interviewers hear the same responses over and over again. The best approach is to tell some very vivid and relevant stories about your past successes that set you apart from the crowd. In telling your success stories remember that the interviewer is most interested in your unique contribution to a problem's resolution. In addition, keep in mind that the stories you choose to tell say something about your record of success, but they also reveal a great deal about what's important to you.

Trigger Story   One of the areas that's always interested me is leadership. Figuring out how to get people to do things and making a group work toward a common end have always been challenging. Ever since I was a kid I took whatever opportunities I could find to play a leadership role. I've been involved with a lot of sports teams and was captain of the track team in both junior high and high school. Once I got into college I decided to pursue academics more than sports—I had some injuries that prevented me from having a strong college career in sports so I didn't want to waste my time. I got involved in politics pretty heavily—I ran for president of the student senate and won two years in a row.

What those experiences did was teach me that I really did like to lead people and that I was pretty good at it. I found that skill and interest transferring into my work life as well. In my first job I became a team leader in my division, and we outperformed the internal competition three years in a row.

The thing that I like most about playing a leadership role is the challenge of figuring out who the people in a particular task group are and what makes them tick. Once I figure out who it is I'm working with and what motivates them, I get a real charge out of harnessing the power of the team.

FACTOR FOUR

Rational Thought Process

One of the most talked-about problems in the contemporary work force is the complaint that today's applicants lack the ability to be critical thinkers. As the marketplace gets more complex, the need to have employees who can solve problems is a priority. Your ability to demonstrate your critical thinking abilities will take you far in the interview process. Being able to articulate what you want in a job and why you think you can handle that sort of work will make the difference between moving ahead or being passed over.

The astute applicant realizes that in addition to gaining information in an interview, the corporate interviewer is also trying to get a feel for the applicant's potential. Conveying to the interviewer that you are an intelligent, resourceful, and highly competent person will take you a long way in the selection process. Demonstrating an ability in the interview to solve problems, or more important, to think in a problem-solving mode, will impress and reassure the interviewer.

The key word here is *process*. As the business world gets more complex and competition more fierce, leaders of corporations realize that what they need most, throughout the organizational ranks, are people who think well. While implementation remains important, it's the "idea people" who make the difference in the long run. Being able to see new angles on old problems is highly valued, as is identifying new problems to be tackled. It's the "tinkerers," says Harvard Business School Professor of Leadership Abraham Zalesnik, who make the difference in the contemporary company. This sentiment is reflected in the number of companies that create opportunities for "intrapreneurs," people whose role it is to think of new products, services, and processes for the organization. In a sense everyone in the successful company of the 1990s needs to be an intrapreneur. The emphasis on each employee being a high-level thinker and problem solver is a notion that's here to stay. As an applicant seeking work with these companies it is to your great advantage to convey an ability to think clearly, creatively, and rationally.

Trigger Story   One of the most challenging situations I've ever been in was when I took a job as a project manager for a small company that had developed a new line of computer software. I had been on the job for about a week when I became extremely frustrated. The president of the company, the person who hired me, had not given me any direction since our initial orientation meeting. I didn't know what I was supposed to do. I decided to go in and tell him of my frustration. We had a brief meeting at which I told him of my frustration over his lack of direction. He told me he hired me because he thought I could figure out the best way to apply my talents to the task at hand. If he'd made a mistake, he offered, we could go our separate ways and there would be no hard feelings.

After getting over the shock of almost losing my week-old job, I told him that there was no problem and that I would get going right away. I decided that the best thing I could do was figure out what needed to be done most with this product and do it—fast. I spoke with the software designers and found out that the product was ready to go to production, but that they had no idea how many to produce, they had no packaging for it, and they didn't have any marketing plans. I got hold of a planning program I had used before and developed a time line for production, design, and marketing of the product. I did some market research, spoke with some advertisers, and made some decisions on a first run of the product. Once my system was in place I found myself with plenty to do and an organized strategy for doing it.

After that things worked out very well and my tenure with that company was quite successful—and I never again asked the president what he wanted me to do.

FACTOR FIVE

Maturity

There is a lot of talk these days about the lack of maturity of the emerging work force. The *New York Times* recently had an article that reported on the number of people in their 20s and 30s who were returning home to live with parents. Although some gave economics as their reason for this retreat, a large number gave responses that led the researchers to believe it was not economics but the inability to cope with the demands of modern life that brought them back home.

Imagine the worry of the corporate recruiter who reads that article. The thought of hiring someone who is living with Mom and Dad to avoid the harsh realities of life in the 1990s would send shivers up one's spine.

There is a perception, articulated in popular books, movies, and other media, that growing up is a problem for the current generation. There is in fact a concern that prolonged adolescence is a result of a generation raised in an affluent society, and that for many college has served as a way of perpetuating the irresponsibility of an entire generation.

Recruiters, burned by seemingly attractive prospects who leave a company after a few months because they can't stand the stress, are aware of the maturity problem. In seeking talent, they are increasingly concerned that the people they pick are "grown up" enough to handle the territory.

The best way to demonstrate that you have the maturity to survive the inevitable difficulties and challenges of life in corporate America is to convey to your interviewer your sense of responsibility. Highlighting past experiences that demonstrate your willingness and ability to "hang in" during difficult times will help immensely. Demonstrating your willingness and ability to act as a leader and to gain others' confidence in your leadership can also help tremendously. Remember, those doing the hiring don't want to raise you; they want to benefit from your having been raised well.

Trigger Story   One of the most personally satisfying things I've done was to help set up a crisis center in college. The idea began when some friends and I were sitting around in the dormitory. A guy down the hall was having a difficult time—we didn't know if it was a drug problem, an emotional problem, or what, but he clearly needed some help. After searching for some help on campus and off, we realized that there were no crisis services available for people in need of them. We went to the campus counseling center and asked them what if anything could be done about it. They said that they would be glad to help but that there were no funds. We went to the dean of students and told him of our concern. He was very responsive and supportive and even gave us a room and a little money to get started. With the help of the counseling center we got some outside experts to come in and meet with us. Since money was scarce we decided to try a peer counseling approach. We recruited interested students and got the experts to train us at minimal cost. Eventually we set up a 24-hour drop-in center with a crisis hotline. We did some peer counseling and a lot of referral to outside agencies. The best part about it was that we now had a place that people could come any time for immediate help until they could get to a professional. The center was very successful and has become a well-known place on campus. In recent years I have volunteered to help new students become peer counselors. I spend a couple of weekends a year each September getting the place up and running—it's a lot of fun.

FACTOR SIX

Planning and Organization

As organizations continue to reduce the ranks of management, the ability for every employee to perform managerial tasks becomes essential. As organizational hierarchies flatten out, leaving fewer middle-level managers to oversee the work, the expectation is that successful employees can manage their own work. The ability to plan and organize one's responsibilities and to monitor one's own performance is a trait greatly valued by those doing the hiring. The extent to which an applicant can demonstrate in an interview the skills involved in planning and organizing projects will determine the interviewer's sense that the applicant can handle a high level of responsibility.

There are many approaches to planning that make sense. The important thing in an interview is to have an approach. This approach should include a clear strategy for analyzing problems, setting goals and objectives, creating strategies for solving problems, implementing plans, and evaluating results. Being careful to comment on each of these key variables will assure your interviewer that you understand and are capable of engaging in the planning process. Being able to articulate clearly each of the elements of the planning process will assure the interviewer that you have an organized mind and are capable of organized activity.

Trigger Story In my last job I was asked to command the computerization of the organization's business office. It wasn't officially part of my job but I was the person in the organization who knew the most about computer systems. I was asked to manage the transition with the understanding that it would take about 20 percent of my time until completed. I was excited about the project and committed to making it as smooth a transition as possible. Since management was committed to getting the best system possible, money was no object. My two concerns were getting the best equipment and getting the people affected through the transition with as little difficulty as possible. I knew that it would take careful planning to execute the plan smoothly.

The first thing I did was to poll the office staff to find out what their needs were and what their concerns were about the transition to computers. At the same time I had representatives from the top computer companies come in and pitch their products to me. After gathering all this information I spent some time with it, made some decisions, and drafted a proposal to management that included product choices, installation time lines, training time lines, and project completion target dates.

Once management accepted my plan I presented it to the office staff and asked for their input. I then made modifications in the plan, ran it by management one more time, and implemented it. The installation of the system, the training, and the total transition went on as scheduled with only a few minor glitches. A month after the shift was completed I did an informal survey with the office staff to see how things were going and how they felt about the transition. I was happy to see that almost all the staff felt the changes had increased their productivity and that they felt comfortable with the new system.

FACTOR SEVEN

Reaction to Pressure

Because of increased global competition, most U.S. corporations believe that to remain on top they must constantly be outdoing their competitors. The typical response of the vice president when confronted with a major success by a subordinate is "Yes, but what are you going to do for us tomorrow?" In the progressive company there is no room for resting on one's laurels. Too many organizations have gone under or lost ground by getting arrogant about their success. The successful companies and the successful employees in those companies recognize that in the accelerated pace of the contemporary marketplace, innovation and change are constants.

Because of these conditions, those doing the hiring are seeking people who not only can handle the pressure but also have ways of managing that pressure and, at best, can thrive on it. While you can count on getting some questions on your reactions to pressure and change, it's to your advantage to discuss that aspect of modern professional life before your interviewer brings it up. As discussed later in this book, it is clear that if you are bothered by pressure or change, the corporate world is not for you. Taking a positive stance on this issue early in an interview can serve you well. Showing that you can stand the heat, and may even welcome it, gives you an edge over others who merely demonstrate an ability to tolerate it.

Although no one serious about getting high-prestige offers will admit to not liking pressure, taking an aggressive position on this issue can enhance your stature in the eyes of the interviewer.

Trigger Story   One of the most stressful situations I was ever in was when I worked for a small distribution company. We were telemarketing a piece of computer software that was unique. However, word was out in the industry that another company was developing a similar product to compete with ours, but it wouldn't be out for another month. The president of the company decided that the month we had prior to the release of the competitor's product could be very lucrative. He decided to hire 50 temporary people to market our software aggressively. Since I was in charge of distribution and knew the most about marketing the product, he put me in charge of hiring and training the temporary staff.

Finding people who were willing to learn to market a product for just one month was difficult. I tapped all the employment agencies in the area and developed an incentive program with bonuses for high sales. I then hired and trained the 50 operators to market and place orders. Within ten days we had our 50 people up and running. It was an intense period for me but very exciting. After a month we had met our quota. There was also an interesting break. The competition fell behind on its time line and couldn't release its product for an additional six weeks. We were able to retain 40 of the people we had originally hired for the additional six weeks and managed to outsell our initial projections by 50 percent.

SUMMARY

In this chapter we have presented an outline of the various factors that are key to the evaluation of candidates seeking work in corporate America. We have also given you examples of achievements that reflect strengths in each of the categories. Taken together these guidelines and examples form a profile of the ideal candidate. If you see yourself in all, or at least in most, of the factors, your chances of getting an interesting position in the corporate sector are good. If there are aspects you feel weak in, you may want to develop those sides of yourself. If you find three or more of the key characteristics unappealing, you may want to consider work in a less demanding environment. In the next chapter we will discuss types of questions used by interviewers to rate a candidate's ranking in the seven categories, as well as responses that could help or hinder your chances. Before moving to the next chapter complete Power Prep Strategy II, which will help strengthen your performance in each key area.

POWER PREP STRATEGY II

Each of the seven key evaluation factors is critical to your interview performance. The following activities will help you clarify your strengths in each area, compensate for your weaknesses, and help you identify the stories that match each area. Your personal trigger stories, like the ones presented in this chapter, can make the difference between your being seen as an average candidate and as an outstanding one.

Aggressiveness and Enthusiasm

What can you do to be an aggressive candidate and how can you demonstrate your aggressiveness in this interview? _____

_____

_____

What genuine enthusiasm do you have for this organization, its products and/or services, and the job itself? _____

_____

_____

What is your best story to demonstrate that you are an aggressive employee? _____

_____

_____

What is your best story to show what you can do when you're enthusiastic about a product or service? _____

_____

_____

Communication Skills

Rate the following communication skills from 1 to 10, 1 being your strongest, 10 being your weakest:

_____ Listening

_____ Public speaking

_____ Report writing

_____ Letter writing

_____ Creative writing

_____ Debating

_____ Summarizing

_____ Networking

_____ Selling

_____ Negotiating

Next, take the three lowest-rated categories (items 8, 9, and 10) and consider ways to improve that area (for example, practice listening or read a book on public speaking).

Item 8 _____ Strategy for improvement _____

_____

_____

Item 9 _____ Strategy for improvement _____

_____

_____

Item 10 _____ Strategy for improvement _____

_____

_____

Record of Success

List the five achievements in your work life of which you are proudest and describe the unique role you played in bringing about a successful outcome.

Achievement 1 _____

Your contribution _____

Achievement 2 _____

Your contribution _____

Achievement 3 _____

Your contribution _____

Achievement 4 _____

Your contribution _____

Achievement 5 _____

Your contribution _____

Rational Thought Process

Which of the following thought processes do you handle well? Assign each item a rating from 1 to 5, 1 being weak, 3 being moderate, and 5 being strong:

Clarifying problems   1 2 3 4 5

Evaluation alternatives   1 2 3 4 5

Generating solutions   1 2 3 4 5

Testing ideas   1 2 3 4 5

Determining outcomes   1 2 3 4 5

For each of the items you rated 4 or 5, write a brief description of a time when you used that skill effectively. For each of the items you circled 1, 2, or 3, write a way you might strengthen that skill (for example, practice brainstorming or a technique for generating solutions).

Clarifying problems (rating _____) _____

_____

_____

Evaluating alternatives (rating _____) _____

_____

_____

Generating solutions (rating _____) _____

_____

_____

Testing ideas (rating _____) _____

_____

_____

Determining outcomes (rating _____) _____

_____

_____

Maturity

If you were to set your age, not by chronological date, but by level of maturity, how old would you now be? _____

If you chose an age older than your actual age, what evidence can you present? If you chose an age younger than your actual age, what can you do to present yourself as more mature than you think you are. List three experiences that address your level of maturity in a positive light.

Work experience _____

Family experience _____

Social experience _____

Planning and Organization

What is the most elaborate project you ever organized? What was your role in the project? _____

_____

_____

There are many ways to plan; however, there are key components essential to every planning process. Keep the following steps in mind and use them in your interview to show you have an organized mind capable of comprehensive planning. A comprehensive planning process includes

Mission or purpose.   What is it you are trying to achieve?

Goals.   What are your long-term targets that will serve your purpose?

Objectives.   What specific aims do you have to reach your goals?

Plans/Strategies.   What will you do to fulfill your objectives?

Activities.   Who is going to implement which parts of the plan, when, and how?

Evaluation.   How are you going to judge the success of the venture?

Integrate the preceding six steps of a comprehensive planning process into your presentation of your planning and organizing skills and your interviewer will leave the interview confident in your planning and organizing abilities.

Reaction to Pressure

Interviews are by design stressful situations. Each of us reacts to stress differently. In what ways do your body and your behavior respond to stress? Some frequently reported examples are sweaty hands, backache, and talking too fast. A stress reaction can kill an interview. What are the typical things that happen to you when you get nervous and what can you do to compensate?

Examples: Sweaty hands: Arrive early and wash hands.

Talking too fast: Focus on speed of speech and slow down periodically.

Take a moment and list three reactions that your body and behavior have to stress and your strategies to combat them.

Reaction 1 _____   Strategy _____

Reaction 2 _____   Strategy _____

Reaction 3 _____   Strategy _____

Interviewers are also looking for evidence that you can handle stress on the job. Describe three incidents from work situations in which you handled stress well.

Incident 1 _____

_____

_____

Incident 2 _____

_____

_____

Incident 3 _____

_____

_____

You've just completed a series of exercises that will fine-tune your ability to perform optimally in each of the seven key evaluation factors. Review this material before your next interview and you will dazzle the interviewer with your competence—and your ability to demonstrate it.

3

Winning Answers to Key Questions

Each of the seven evaluation factors presented in the previous chapter carries with it some key questions. Your answers to the questions in each category will influence your rating in that category and ultimately your chances in the interview. This chapter presents an overview of the questions that reveal information about a candidate for each category and includes responses and response strategies that could either enhance or hinder your chances.

The responses presented for each of the questions are not intended to be a script. The intention is to provide the gist of what a good answer would be. It's important to remember that your responses should match your identity. If your answers ring true you're much more likely to be viewed as a viable candidate.

The questions in this chapter are derived from the audiotape "How Do They Decide" developed by the Xsell Team and based on thousands of interviews with Fortune 500 recruiters and executives. Each question will be analyzed to help the reader understand its significance and the type of information likely to be culled from it. Next, responses to each question will be given that are considered by the experts to be appropriate (Winner Answers) and inappropriate (Killer Answers). Each response will be followed by a critique. Since it is just as important to know what not to say in an interview, we urge you to read and consider the Killer Answers as well as the Winner Answers.

CATEGORY ONE: AGGRESSIVENESS AND ENTHUSIASM

This category is essential since successful companies depend on a work force that is highly aggressive and enthusiastic. Your energy level and commitment to the task at hand will be measured by your responses in this category, as will your ability to convey a sense of excitement and a willingness to ''go the extra mile'' for the company.

Aggressiveness here concerns your willingness to apply your skills and talents in an assertive and hard-driving way. Organizations seeking new employees, regardless of their rank, role, or area of expertise, want people who believe their own function is critical to the organization and warrants a diligent approach. Similarly, they are looking for people whose enthusiasm for the organization and its products and services is unbridled.

QUESTION 1

Why do you feel you can be successful in this position?

Analysis A fairly open-ended question, this item provides an opportunity for the applicant to demonstrate a sense of excitement and challenge. The response to the question will give the interviewer key information on the applicant's drive and self-confidence in relation to this position.

Killer Answer I don't know; I'm pretty good at most things I do. If I get offered this job and decide to take it I'm sure I could rise to the occasion. I've always been successful in the past.

Critique Although this may on the surface sound like an acceptable response it is lacking in several ways. First, the language is weak. Phrases such as "I don't know" and "pretty good" do not reflect the sort of aggressiveness required to break into the best companies. Further, lumping this position with everything else the applicant has ever done dilutes the person's success and real enthusiasm for this particular position. Finally, the suggestion that the applicant might not take the position once offered also reflects a lack of enthusiasm.

Winner Answer Given my history, this is the perfect position at this point in my career. I have been studying this field and watching your organization for several years in anticipation of such an opportunity. I have the requisite skills [tell a brief story to prove it]. I am in a perfect position to take this job and really run with it.

Critique This is a strong response because it tells the interviewer the applicant has both the skill and the knowledge to do the job. The story illustrating the applicant's skill reinforces the initial statement. Finally, the applicant's intention to "run with it" supports the desired enthusiasm and aggressiveness.

QUESTION 2

What is your greatest strength and weakness, and how will these affect your performance here?

Analysis The biggest danger with this question is that it is really two questions in one, plus a follow-up. The two pitfalls here are taking the part about strengths not seriously enough, and taking the part about weaknesses too seriously. It is important to remember that your responses will not only inform the interviewer of your assets and liabilities but also present a broad view of your values and your sense of self worth.

Killer Answer In terms of strengths, I really can't pinpoint one thing in particular that stands out. I think my skills are pretty well rounded. As far as weaknesses go, I guess I get bored if a project drags on too long.

Critique The biggest problem with this response is that the applicant essentially refuses to answer the first part of the question. The response to the second part hints at a potential lack of enthusiasm. Finally, the responses to the first two parts of the question leave the applicant with little chance for a respectable response to the third part.

Winner Answer In terms of strengths, I believe my greatest asset is that I have a highly organized mind, capable of creating order out of confusion. My greatest weakness perhaps is that I have little patience for people who don't value the same sense of order that I do. I believe my organizational skills can help this organization achieve its goals more quickly, and that my appreciation for streamlining complex problems can sometimes rub off on my co-workers.

Critique This response does three important things. It clearly identifies the applicant's greatest strength. It identifies a weakness that really could just as easily be perceived as a strength. Finally, it points out the benefits of the applicant's strength and weakness both to the organization and to other employees.

QUESTION 3

Have you ever been put on the spot by a professor or advisor when you've felt unsure of yourself? How did you respond?

Analysis   This question probes an applicant's ability to work in unfamiliar territory. It is designed to get a picture of the applicant's willingness and ability to tackle assignments that are a stretch beyond current levels of competence.

Killer Answer   I believe it's important to question authority. If I learned anything in school it's that a lot of professors think they have all the answers when they're really out of touch with what's happening in the real world. You know, all that ivory tower stuff.

Critique   The biggest problem with this response is that it shifts the focus away from the applicant. Serious interviewers are not interested in your opinion of higher education. Rather, they want to know how you handle yourself in the situation presented in the question. The other real problem with this response is that it creates doubts in the interviewer's mind about your willingness to follow instructions.

Winner Answer   I tried to make the most of my years in school, so I often took courses in areas I was unfamiliar with. Consequently I often got challenged by my professors. Whenever I found myself in a situation where I knew less than I might about a subject I tried to anticipate the questions, so that I'd be prepared to respond. When challenged I'd try to make as educated a guess as possible, acknowledge what I didn't know, and take it from there. For example [give an illustration if you have one], . . .

Critique   The strongest thing about this response is that it articulates the applicant's willingness to deal with difficult situations. It also shows that the applicant has ambition and a clear sense of how to approach novel and ambiguous problems.

QUESTION 4

Have you ever received a grade lower than you expected? If so, what did you do about it?

Analysis   In addition to revealing information about the applicants' enthusiasm and aggressiveness, responses to this question reveal information about their sense of fairness and willingness to fight for their cause.

Killer Answer   I remember one time I thought I deserved a B and got a C. I went to the instructor and he showed me the breakdown of the grades—I was on the border but clearly in the C category. I was glad I checked it out rather than just accept it at face value.

Critique   This answer starts out strong but ends with a dramatic fizzle. It looks as if the applicant is committed to following through at first. Then it becomes clear he or she lacks the drive to create change.

Winner Answer   I had a horrible experience once with an earth science professor. The man was known for his bias toward science majors, which I was not. There was a large group of nonmajors in the class who felt he had unrealistic expectations about our knowledge base. Many of the students did poorly as a result of his bias. While I did okay I joined the other students in issuing a statement to the department head suggesting there be a review of the way the course was presented.

Critique   This response demonstrates the applicant's ability to overcome a difficult situation and come out on top. It also indicates a high level of commitment to a sense of fairness. Finally it exhibits the applicant's willngness to get involved for the benefit of the group, beyond the level of self-interest.

QUESTION 5

For job advancement would you consider an advanced degree?

Analysis   This is a simple question designed to gauge your ambition and to see if your own level of investment in your future dictates an investment in you by the company.

Killer Answer   I don't know; I've got my BA in management and I think I got a pretty good education. I think real world experience is far more valuable than anything you learn in school.

Critique   Although this response attempts to show the applicant in a positive light and indirectly to flatter the interviewer (who is part of "the real world"), it speaks poorly of the applicant's willingness to better himself or herself. Consequently the applicant conveys, at best, a lack of ambition and, at worst, arrogance.

Winner Answer   I learned a lot as an undergraduate and would certainly consider an advanced degree for the right reasons. I'd want to be careful though; I think a lot of people go back to school for the wrong reasons. If I found I was doing work I really valued and I needed more education to excel in that area I certainly wouldn't hesitate.

Critique   This response shows ambition, enthusiasm, and drive. It also shows that the applicant has a discriminating mind and is careful about making major career decisions.

QUESTION 6

What competitive activities have you participated in? Were these worthwhile?

Analysis This question gets at your comfort with and confidence in competition by probing your history with structured competitive situations. It is a perfect opportunity to discuss any team activities or organized efforts in which competition was a key factor.

Killer Answer I'm a highly competitive person by nature. I think I take a competitive slant on virtually everything I do. After all, that's how you survive in the corporate jungle, isn't it?

Critique This person has been doing too much reading about sharks and Huns. Although the corporate world is a highly competitive arena, those involved in it resent the image that they are a bunch of seething barracudas.

Winner Answer I like team sports and participate in them as often as I can. I used to play a lot of basketball and still do when I get a chance. The thrill of working with a team toward a common end and outperforming the competition can be really thrilling.

Critique This response suggests that the applicant has a healthy view of competition. The implication is that he or she would use competitive energy to outdo the competition, not to undo the work of colleagues.

CATEGORY TWO: COMMUNICATION SKILLS

I met a man last week who ran a video production business. In the course of our meeting I learned that he had a Ph.D. in physics and used to teach at the college level. When he found out that I worked with career changers for a living, he said, ''It's easy to change careers these days. All you need is to be able to write well and know how to talk to people.'' While I'm not sure it's quite as simple as that, the point that communication skills are crucial to the successful job seeker cannot be overstated. Because questions in this category address your ability to communicate, they are the questions most likely to be used to judge your actual skill in this area. This is the one category in which interviewers get to see the applicants in action, not just hear about their performance. Therefore, it is one of those categories that can make you or break you. Anyone who has done any teaching, training, or sales presentations knows that the more you do it, the better it comes across. That's why we strongly urge you to practice your responses to the 50 questions in this chapter before an interview. There's a good chance that your ability to communicate effectively will have a major impact on the number and types of offers you get. The following questions are designed to determine an applicant's ability to communicate effectively.

QUESTION 7

How do you go about influencing someone to accept your ideas?

Analysis   The response to this question will tell the interviewer, first, how comfortable you are with the notion of influencing others, and second, how able you are in this area.

Killer Answer   I usually depend on the value of the idea. If it's a good idea and the people I'm dealing with are reasonable, I generally don't have much trouble getting my ideas accepted.

Critique   The problem with this response is that it doesn't address the real problem, which is how you deal with people who don't think your idea is a good one. This response suggests that the applicant is only willing to work in a harmonious situation, not in a discordant one.

Winner Answer   That's something I've worked very hard on over the years. At some point I realized that good ideas, even great ideas, sometimes don't get received that way. I now appreciate the fact that the way you present an idea is just as important as the idea itself. When trying to influence people I usually try to put myself in their position and think about their perspective. I'm then able to present thoughts to them in a way more likely to end in success.

Critique   This response demonstrates the applicant's appreciation for the complexity of interpersonal communication and the difficulty in getting others to change their minds. The applicant conveys an understanding of the importance of strategy when influencing someone and articulates a reasoned approach. Finally, the applicant demonstrates an understanding of the importance of form as well as substance when communicating under difficult circumstances.

QUESTION 8

What experience have you had in making oral presentations? How do you rate your skills in this area?

Analysis This question is intended to discern the applicant's comfort in public speaking and to gain the applicant's self-assessment of his or her skill.

Killer Answer I think everyone gets nervous making presentations. I can do them, but to tell you the truth people don't always listen. Sometimes, I think it's better just to give people the information on paper and then answer questions.

Critique This answer clearly places the applicant at the bottom of the pool. It not only suggests discomfort with oral presentations but also implies that it is not even an area that necessarily needs development.

Winner Answer I read somewhere that public speaking was the number one fear of people in this country. After I read that I figured that if most people are so scared of it, harnessing my own fear and mastering the skill of oral presentation would probably put me strides ahead of the competition. So I do presentations every chance I get and find that the more I do them the more comfortable I get—and the better I get.

Critique This is a strong response because it comments specifically on the applicant's competence in this area and shows that the applicant is working on further developing an important skill. By acknowledging that oral presentations are tricky, the applicant demonstrates a willingness to be honest and candid as well.

QUESTION 9

How would you compare your verbal skills to your writing skills?

Analysis   This is what I call a booby-trapped question. Whenever you get a question that asks you to compare two things, beware. The question is designed to get you to speak about your weaknesses.

Killer Answer   [Any response that says why you're better at one skill or the other.]

Critique   You took the bait.

Winner Answer   It seems as if organizations are more dependent than ever on the ability of employees to be articulate both orally and in writing. I am constantly taking advantage of opportunities to develop my oral and written communication skills. These days I think they're vital competencies for anyone expecting to be successful in the business world.

Critique   This response avoids the trap of being seen as weak in either area and demonstrates the applicant's understanding of the importance of strong communication skills. Most important it reassures the interviewer that the applicant is someone who has a solid base of generic skills that can be drawn on regardless of the direction the organization takes.

QUESTION 10

What do you least like about writing a term paper?

Analysis   This question probes your willingness to do research, uncover information, and come up with answers to difficult questions.

Killer Answer   The worst thing is when it's on a topic I'm really not interested in. I don't mind doing the research if its interesting stuff, but so often there was never any real world application to the material being researched.

Critique   Although many readers may be nodding their heads in agreement with this response, it leaves the interviewer uneasy. Often a job may require tasks that are mundane and tedious. Hearing an applicant state a dislike for anything not interesting is unsettling.

Winner Answer   If I'm doing a good job on it I'm probably discovering that there is an unlimited amount of information available on a subject. The task I find most difficult is deciding when I've obtained enough data to stop researching and start writing.

Critique   This response demonstrates the applicant's understanding of and willingness to do research. It shows an ability to uncover in-depth information and suggests that the applicant is competent in this area.

QUESTION 11

How should supervisors and subordinates interact?

Analysis   This question is designed to discover the applicant's approach to communication in the organizational hierarchy. The response is likely to indicate an applicant's level of skill in a potentially complex area.

Killer Answer   I like to think that we can be friends. After all if you're going to work closely with someone you might as well get to know that person. That way everyone understands each other and you can avoid a lot of unnecessary conflict.

Critique   The worst thing about this response is that it demonstrates a high level of immaturity. Anyone the least bit knowledgeable about relationships in the workplace knows that conflict is an inevitable part of working life. The notion that creating close friendships can simplify things shows a real lack of understanding of the relationship between work and personal boundaries.

Winner Answer   I believe that clear communication throughout the hierarchy of an organization is critical to the organization's thriving. I'd like to think I've developed good strong skills in that area. In terms of superior-subordinate relationships I think it's most important to realize that each person and each relationship is different. The best approach for me is to begin with no assumptions and see how the relationship evolves over time.

Critique   This answer indicates an understanding of the complexity of interpersonal communication and the diversity of human relationships. The applicant clearly articulates the importance of strong communication skills and conveys confidence in this area.

QUESTION 12

How would you be described by a close friend?

Analysis   This question is designed to shed some light on an applicant's character. It's one of those questions that seems to have nothing to do with an applicant's potential, but it reflects a trend in business for hiring people with high personal standards as well as strong skills.

Killer Answer   I think people would say I'm a fun person to be with. The best way to describe me is I like to work hard and play hard.

Critique   Although this response may sound entirely positive to some of you, it raises several problems. First, it does not answer the question, leaving the interviewer wondering whether the applicant has any close relationships. In addition it leaves the interviewer wondering about the nature of "play hard" and raises some potentially damaging questions, for example, those concerning drug or alcohol abuse.

Winner Answer   My friends are very important to me. The most important aspect of my relationship with them is the sense that we can rely on each other. We're all very busy so there are times we don't see each other that often. With the few people I would call close friends it's knowing that we're there for each other that counts.

Critique   This response reflects a sense of maturity, so much a concern in today's corporate world. The applicant's commitment to high standards and to a few key people suggests that the individual is well balanced. It also rings true. Don't use it if it's not—it won't work.

QUESTION 13

How do you get along with co-workers?

Analysis   The response to this question, along with the previous ones on superior-subordinate relationships and friendships, gives the interviewer an overall impression of your ability to communicate effectively. In a sense it is the most critical of the communication questions because 80 percent of the people who leave their jobs, according to the department of labor, do so because they don't fit in with the other people. Your ability to communicate your effectiveness in peer relationships will help ease the interviewer's concern that you may be yet another bad match.

Killer Answer   I get along with most everyone. I'm an easygoing kind of person. I've never really met anyone that I couldn't get along with. Once in a while everyone meets someone that they don't like as much as the rest of the staff, but I try to overlook that. If someone is really obnoxious they usually don't last anyway—so I wait it out, knowing that eventually they'll disappear.

Critique   Although this response, like some of the other Killer Answers, seems fairly harmless, it has several problems. First, no one gets along with everyone. After making this broad statement the interviewee then goes on to talk about people that he or she doesn't like, making the response sound somewhat contradictory. Finally, the interviewee breaks the cardinal rule of interviewing—never say negative things about other people.

Winner Answer   I generally get along very well with co-workers. Occasionally I might run into a conflict with someone. When that happens I usually focus on what the conflict is about rather than on personalities. I find that that approach helps me maintain a respectful relationship with anyone—and often leads to resolution and strengthened relationships.

Critique   This response suggests that the applicant is a well-balanced person, possessing a high level of human relations skills. By making the distinction between problems and personalities, the applicant appears to be someone who has worked out problems in the past and has a history of successful interpersonal relationships.

CATEGORY THREE: RECORD OF SUCCESS

Your record of success is your most important credential for gaining access to the best companies. Effectively conveying a view of yourself as a person with an impressive track record will do more for your chances than any other single tactic. Careful review of the questions in this category will help arm you for your campaign.

There are two tacks you can take here, depending on the material you have to work with and the job you're applying for. If your background vividly illustrates your ability to do the job in question, you merely need to choose the best examples and present them.

If however, your record of success has no apparent relationship to the job, your task becomes one of education as well as illustration. If the interviewer has an appreciation for the transferability of skills, all you need do is make the connection between the examples you choose to talk about and the job in question. Some interviewers, however, like some applicants, will not see the link between history and potential future. What you must do then is point out how your past relates to what the company needs. By showing that the skills you've used in the past are directly transferable and applicable to the tasks required on the job in question, you allay any fears and, if done well, effectively plead your case.

QUESTION 14

What do you consider to be your most significant accomplishment and why?

Analysis   This question gives the interviewer insight into your values. What you choose to talk about in response will reveal a great deal about your standards and priorities.

Killer Answer   Just making it through school was tough. You know I worked my way through school. I'm proud of having been able to juggle studies and work at the same time.

Critique   On the surface this may seem like a good answer; many of you have probably used it, although it falls short in several ways. First, it is fairly common today for students to work their way through school, so there's nothing unique about it. Second, it's too general, focusing on an ongoing process rather than a specific activity that highlights your uniqueness.

Winner Answer   [Rather than give you a specific line of thought to work with, I suggest you need to think of something you've done that highlights your uniqueness. Some examples: Won first prize in a math competition, was elected class officer, managed a family crisis, wrote a comprehensive school newspaper article, won a debating contest, rebuilt a car engine from scratch, reorganized a department, successfully launched a new product line.]

Critique   Each of these examples is unique, impressive, and likely to set you apart from the crowd. Remember that you don't necessarily need to have received formal recognition for this accomplishment. It has to be something you did extremely well and are proud of. Spend some time thinking about this. It will work much better for you than a generic ''worked my way through school'' response.

QUESTION 15

Under what conditions have you been most successful in any undertaking?

Analysis   This question probes the conditions under which you work best. Your response will reveal information about your preferred way of working, factors that influence your chances of success, and possibly your limitations.

Killer Answer   I can succeed at just about anything I put my mind to. As long as I know what's expected of me, I usually get results.

Critique   Although this too seems like a reasonable response, it has several flaws. As with the previous question, it is what we would call a generic response that leaves a weak impression at best. However, the real problem with this answer is that it presumes the organization is looking for people who are good at following others' directions, not charting their own. In these lean times, most corporations are seeking people who are self-motivated. Communicating that you are someone who needs direction from others can be deadly.

Winner Answer   My approach to problem solving involves a systematic process of gathering relevant information about a problem, clearly identifying the problem, setting a strategy, and then implementing it. I find most people skip the first two parts and jump straight to strategy. As long as I have enough information and a clear view of the problem I can tackle anything.

Critique   This response demonstrates that the applicant has solved difficult problems in the past, has thought about strategy, and has developed a method for solving difficult problems. It also shows a sense of confidence and willingness to use proven skills in the future.

QUESTION 16

How hard do you work to achieve your objectives?

Analysis   The most obvious thing about this question is that the interviewer wants to hear that the applicant is a hard worker. The key here is presenting a response that shows the applicant's willingness and ability to fulfill responsibilities.

Killer Answer   My energy level on a particular task depends on the difficulty of the task and how badly I want to achieve it. If I've decided that something is really important I'll put my all into it and make it happen.

Critique   The first mistake here is the introduction of the idea that the applicant has a limited reservoir of energy. No successful company is interested in anyone who doesn't seem to have unbounded energy. Second, the notion that the applicant works hard only on tasks that he or she is personally committed to suggests an unwillingness to accept less than desirable assignments.

Winner Answer   For me the question is not how hard I work. It's a given that if I've set an objective or if I've been given an important assignment I work as hard as necessary to achieve the desired results. The question for me is how smart do I work—that is, what can I do to make the completion of the task come as easily and smoothly as possible so I can move on to other things.

Critique   The strength of this response is that it suggests that the applicant has unlimited energy and a high level of commitment. It also indicates that the applicant approaches problems in a way to ensure the maximum utilization of his or her resources—what the question was really after.

QUESTION 17

Has competition had any positive or negative impact on your accomplishments? How?

Analysis This question is designed to weed out candidates who are uncomfortable in a competitive environment. The interviewer is looking for the extent to which the applicant feels intimidated by competitive situations.

Killer Answer I like competition. It sometimes gives me the push I need to get going. I never find it overwhelming. It's just a part of life and part of what keeps me going.

Critique Most people will not believe this response for one minute. Also, it seems to patronize, in addition to being difficult to believe. Most people find competition overwhelming at least some of the time. The response also hints at a lack of motivation and the need for competition as a motivating agent.

Winner Answer If I was afraid of competition I wouldn't be applying for a job in a place like this. I know competition is built in. The most important thing to me is knowing the competition and being clear about what it is we're competing for. When I'm in a competitive situation I like to make sure I understand what's at stake. Once I understand the game plan I enjoy competing wholeheartedly.

Critique This response communicates the same positive outlook on competition as the Killer Answer, but without the whitewash. It also demonstrates that the applicant has a clearly defined way of dealing with competition based on his or her prior experience.

QUESTION 18

What do you consider your earning potential to be five years from now?

Analysis   The real meaning behind this question is "Are you ambitious enough for us and do you have far-reaching goals for yourself."

Killer Answer   I'd like to be making $100,000 a year. There are lots of things I want: a nice car, my own house, maybe a boat. I think a hundred grand five years from now would be a good start.

Critique   No comment.

Winner Answer   I believe my talents can earn me a decent living; that's why I'm applying to a prestigious company such as yours. I plan to make enough money to live comfortably and am willing to do what it takes to ensure that I am well paid throughout my career.

Critique   Unlike the previous answer, this applicant has the good sense not to talk in dollar amounts. Unless you're in salary negotiation, naming numbers is highly inappropriate, not to mention tacky. Showing a sense of self-respect gives the interviewer confidence in your value as a worthwhile applicant.

CATEGORY FOUR: RATIONAL THOUGHT PROCESS

We know of a man who was a supervisor at a paper production company. He lost his job when it was discovered that one of the machines he was responsible for had cut seven hours' worth of 8½-×-11 sized paper 8×11½ instead. What cost him his job was not the mistake itself, but the fact that the machine had been retooled that morning. The sensible thing for anyone with that responsibility would be to check and double-check the settings to make sure the measurements are accurate.

It's stories like this that make interviewers pay so much attention to rational thought process. Rational thought process refers to the capability and tendency for a person to think and act in a lucid, careful, and somewhat predictable fashion. The more clear, succinct, and mindful of detail a person seems in an interview, the more likely that person will score well in this category. Although there is no guarantee that rational behavior will follow a display of rational thought process, the interviewer will most likely make judgments in this area based on your response.

Rational thought process is one of those categories that could make the difference in a close interview. If two equally qualified candidates both give acceptable performances in an interview the job would probably go to the one who seemed most succinct and rational. To the interviewer a rational thought process translates to a higher level of productivity, and fewer mistakes on the job.

QUESTION 19

What are the most important characteristics you are looking for in a job and why?

Analysis This question challenges your rational thought process by presenting an open-ended inquiry into your priorities. As important as your response to this question is your ability to demonstrate an understanding of what "a good job" might be.

Killer Answer I want a job that will really showcase my talents, one with high visibility. I like to think that working in a company like yours will set me apart from the crowd.

Critique Aside from portraying the applicant as an egomaniac with a high need for recognition, this response has several other problems. The biggest problem is that it does not address the needs of the employer at all—something every response should do. In addition it leaves the interviewer wondering if the applicant has any understanding whatsoever of the nature of work.

Winner Answer I'm looking for a job that utilizes my strongest skills, such as [name specific skills]. I think it's also important that my role in the organization be clearly tied to the goals of the organization. Ultimately it would also be great to have a job that is at times challenging, one that stretches me beyond my current abilities.

Critique Although fairly brief, this response accomplishes three things: It highlights the applicant's skills, demonstrates the applicant's understanding of the need for relevance in one's job, and shows the applicant's understanding of the importance of change and development.

QUESTION 20

How do you think our company determines success?

Analysis　This question is designed to see what, if anything, the applicant knows about this particular company. It's meant to weed out those not interested enough or those not smart enough to do their homework.

Killer Answer　Well, because you're a highly successful company I imagine you're concerned with staying on top and beating the competition. I'll bet you consider bottom-line results as your key measure of success.

Critique　Although this response may be entirely true, it is too general to have any positive impact. It tells the interviewer nothing of the applicant's interest in and knowledge of the company. A fair assumption would be that the applicant knows nothing about this organization and its goals.

Winner Answer　I've watched your company introduce a series of new products over the past two years. It seems that you take a comprehensive approach to product development and marketing strategy. It seems to me that you would measure success by the extent to which new products became front-runners in their particular market niche.

Critique　Although this response (for the sake of illustration) is not much more specific than the Killer Answer, it does show that the applicant has some understanding of what the company does. The suggestion that being "number one" is important to this organization and is something it has achieved in the past shows a high regard for the organization and its definition of success.

QUESTION 21

What is the most intellectually challenging thing you are looking for in a job and why?

Analysis This question probes your understanding of the need to choose applicants who can think critically. The applicant's response will give the interviewer a glimpse of the applicant's problem-solving capacity.

Killer Answer I'm looking for a job that lets me use what I know. When you go to a good school like I did you learn a lot about the way things should work. It would be great to be able to apply some of that knowledge to a work situation.

Critique Here the applicant misses the point and misinterprets intellectual challenge with prior learning. The response suggests that the applicant has "the answers" rather than the capacity to formulate new answers to unique problems.

Winner Answer I think it's important to be involved in the short- and long-range planning going on in the organization. I'd like to think that wherever I ended up in a company I could be involved in some way with its research and development activities. Knowing and being a part of where an organization is going is the most intellectually challenging aspect of work for me.

Critique This response indicates that the applicant values intellectual challenge and the stretching of personal limits. It also suggests that the applicant is motivated toward learning about the organization's future and making a contribution to its future endeavors.

QUESTION 22

What is the most intellectually challenging thing you have ever done?

Analysis   This question begins to probe the applicant's level of intelligence. It provides the interviewer with a glimpse of the potential problem-solving ability of the applicant.

Killer Answer   Well, that's a tough question. I'm not really an intellectual. I'm more of a hands-on kind of person. I mean what's the point of intellectualizing? I leave that to the professors at the university. I'm more interested in making things happen.

Critique   At this point we'd like to introduce the "flake factor." The preceding answer is the perfect response for illustration. In fact, in terms of the flake factor this response is off the charts. Not only does the applicant berate the interviewer by belittling the question, but also he or she shows a decided inability to think at a high level.

Winner Answer   A couple of summers ago I worked in an insurance company that was switching over to a computerized mail system. I was only summer help, but I was able, because of some of my computer coursework, to help debug the system. It was really exciting because I was learning as I was doing, but in the long run I was able to suggest some changes that were implemented.

Critique   The strength of this response is that it illustrates the applicant's ability to take prior learning, apply it to a new situation, learn from experience, and apply the new learning.

QUESTION 23

How did you determine your career choice?

Analysis   This question is designed to see whether an applicant's choice in pursuing this line of work in this company has any historical origin. Does the person have a career plan or is he or she aimlessly applying for a variety of jobs.

Killer Answer   I've always wanted to work in the corporate world. Ever since I was a kid I've dreamed about becoming at least a vice president in a large company.

Critique   Aside from being hard to believe, this question raises another problem. It suggests that the applicant will be unhappy in anything less than a vice presidency.

Winner Answer   The summer before my senior year I decided it was time to focus on a specific direction. Even though I was a business major I wasn't sure which business I would end up in. I spent some time thinking about my goals, what I was good at, and what I really wanted out of work and decided that the _____ industry was my best bet.

Critique   This response shows that the applicant has done some serious planning, has narrowed his or her focus, and has targeted a direction. The applicant shows an understanding of the importance of personal career planning and demonstrates an ability to make careful personal decisions.

QUESTION 24

What do you consider most valuable, a high salary or job recognition and advancement?

Analysis Here we have the comparison trap again. If you follow the questioner's lead, you lose. Either you choose money over advancement, which is considered tacky and shortsighted, or you run the risk of being viewed as insincere about your indifference to money.

Killer Answer Money's not that important to me. What I want is to make a contribution to my company and to reap the more significant rewards of recognition and advancement.

Critique This response smacks of insincerity, but even worse, it brings into question the applicant's judgment. If money is not that important to this person, why is he or she seeking work in the corporate world, which by definition must be financially motivated. People not interested in money would probably seek work in environments where the money factor is less central.

Winner Answer For me, those things are inseparable. Although I am not obsessive about money, I assume that with success and the advancement and recognition it brings will come greater financial rewards.

Critique This response is honest and to the point without being in poor taste. It reflects the applicant's ambition and the logical consequences of his or her success.

QUESTION 25

Organize your ladder of success and explain this progression.

Analysis   The response to this question reveals the applicant's understanding of how the corporate world operates and the extent to which the applicant's expectations are realistic. The response also indicates something about the applicant's goals and ambitions.

Killer Answer   I'm on the fast track. I'm one of those people who believes that in America hard work pays. I believe that if I choose the right company I can move up the corporate ladder pretty quickly, and ultimately be one of the people running the company. In a first-rate company like this one, that would be success.

Critique   Although this response may at first seem reasonable, it has several problems. It echoes the beliefs of many people in the corporate world, but it does not acknowledge the fact that the way things work is changing. The last sentence is a bit too patronizing. To the astute interviewer this response might sound like Horatio Alger.

Winner Answer   I think that's probably the biggest challenge facing everyone in the career marketplace today. I think companies are changing the way they deal with career ladders in a dramatic way. Consequently, I think people have to do the same. The key I think is finding an organization that can utilize my skills to the fullest extent. Once I find that, I'll do all I can to increase my value to that company. If I'm making an important contribution I believe that career advancement will be an outcome of that success.

Critique   This response demonstrates the applicant's understanding of the changing workplace. It reflects an understanding of the problems companies face in relation to individual productivity. It suggests that the applicant sees personal career development as tied to performance, and it indicates a drive to succeed without any accompanying unrealistic expectations. Finally, it suggests that the employment contract is one entered into in good faith by both employer and employee.

QUESTION 26

What qualities are most important to determine whom you would hire for this position?

Analysis   By turning the tables on the applicant, this question probes his or her understanding of the needs and requirements of the position. It tells the interviewer the extent to which the applicant understands the demands of the position and the priorities of the organization.

Killer Answer   I would hire someone like me! I'm hard working, intelligent, and motivated. That's what you need in a position like this—someone who's really hungry.

Critique   In this response the applicant fails to take the interviewer's challenge and move beyond the focus on himself or herself. The result is a decided inability to see the overall picture. The response also makes the applicant seem desperate for work—a serious disadvantage.

Winner Answer   I think the 1990s offer some real challenges for corporations. If I were doing the hiring, regardless of the position, I would look for several things. I'd want somebody who wasn't afraid to make decisions, yet was a team player. I'd want someone who appreciated the implications of global competition, yet wasn't intimidated by a world market. Finally, I'd want someone who realized that quality and service are the keys to a company's success.

Critique   In a brief yet direct way the applicant demonstrates an ability to see and understand the employer's needs. By focusing on teamwork, decision making, the world market, quality, and service, the applicant presents a clear view of the priorities of many in the corporate world of the 1990s.

QUESTION 27

What are some of the most creative things you have done?

Analysis   In addition to obviously probing for examples of creativity, this question also investigates what aspects of creativity the applicant most values.

Killer Answer   When I was in high school I had a pretty big role in a class play. Actually I did a lot of acting in high school. I'd say that was my most creative period.

Critique   Here the applicant makes the classic mistake of equating the word *creativity* with traditional creative activities. Unfortunately, most interviewers see little applicable relationship between creative endeavors and creative problem solving on the job.

Winner Answer   One of my most creative periods was when I helped a friend run for student union president at college. Essentially I was responsible for running her campaign, which meant creating a platform on which to run, developing strategies for campaigning, and coming up with ways to increase our support base. For example, one thing we did was run free coffeehouses, where students could hear good music and find out about our positions. It was a very creative period in my life because we were constantly trying to find new angles to pursue.

Critique   The strength of this response lies in its application of creative skills to a complex situation. The applicant portrays the ability to approach a multifaceted task in a creative, problem-solving way. By giving a specific example, the applicant demonstrates the capacity to be a creative problem solver.

QUESTION 28

Do you agree that grade point average is an indication of how successful you would be in this company?

Analysis   This question actually has two purposes. If the applicant did well in school the interviewer is searching for an understanding that workplace success is different from academic success. If the applicant did poorly in school the interviewer is looking to see if there's a problem with the individual's problem-solving capacity.

Killer Answer (for someone with poor grades)   I don't know, look at Dan Quayle, he certainly did okay for himself—and with a C average. I don't think grades mean that much.

Killer Answer (for someone with good grades)   Yes, I think if you can make it in a tough school as I did, it's an indication that you can succeed in the workplace.

Critique   The first response is clearly meant to be distracting and is totally inappropriate. It also brings politics into the process, which can backfire.

The second response shows arrogance and suggests a lack of understanding of the difference between academic and workplace problems.

Winner Answer (for someone with poor grades)   I think it's important that someone show the capacity to get good grades. If a person had a poor track record in every subject it might make me nervous. However, not everyone is going to be committed to excelling in every subject. The important thing from my perspective is that there be some highlights in an individual's academic career that point to potential.

Winner Answer (for someone with good grades)   While managing an academic career is less complex than a demanding job, I do believe there is a correlation. To me the most important thing about a strong academic record is that it reflects a commitment to excellence.

Critique   Both responses in this section frame the person's situation in a positive way: the first by pointing out that there was some successful academic work, the second by pointing to the commitment to excellence. Both responses effectively speak in the third person, thus removing the danger of seeming overly apologetic or arrogant.

QUESTION 29

If you could construct your own job within our organization, what factors would you include?

Analysis   This question is aimed at the applicant's understanding of the complexity of the contemporary workplace. Its intent is to understand the applicant's appreciation for the need to hire people who can make a range of contributions.

Killer Answer   The most important thing to me is making sure that my role is clear and that expectations are realistic. Too many people get burned, I think, when one day they find out they're not as valued as they thought they were.

Critique   This response paints a picture of a fearful employee, looking over his or her shoulder while waiting for the ax to fall. It does little to convey the applicant's understanding of the importance of having employees who can meet diverse organizational needs.

Winner Answer   First, I'd want it to be a job that could use my strongest skills, specifically [mention specific skills]. I'd also want it to be a judgment job, one that was really necessary to meet the goals of the organization. Ideally it would also be one that allowed for some growth and diversification in the future.

Critique   This response demonstrates the applicant's understanding that a good match involves hiring someone whose skills are needed, whose function is clear, and whose potential is great. It leaves the interviewer with a sense that the applicant would most likely make a rich contribution if chosen.

CATEGORY FIVE: MATURITY

As organizations struggle to find the most responsible and conscientious employees, the need for applicants to demonstrate a high level of maturity becomes crucial to the successful interview. The applicant needs to keep in mind that interviewers are looking for mature, highly developed individuals.

Here maturity implies a perspective that tolerates the ambiguity and uncertainty that anyone with major responsibility faces at work. Applicants confronted with the maturity issue must be able to convey their capacity to think and act in a highly responsible fashion. The key here is convincing the interviewer of your ability to see the whole picture and make judgments that reflect sound thinking.

QUESTION 30

In what ways have you been a leader?

Analysis Leadership potential is one of the most highly valued traits in the corporate world today. The applicant's response to this question can go a long way in the campaign for a job offer.

Killer Answer Some people are born leaders and I think I'm one of them. I don't think leadership is a quality you can teach. Either you have it or you don't.

Critique Aside from raising the fatal swelled head again, this response falls short in several other ways. It does not say anything substantive about the applicant, and it implies that this person would not contribute to the leadership potential of other people in the organization.

Winner Answer I've had several jobs where I've played a leadership role, responsible for seeing that jobs get done, and I've always had successful outcomes. More important though, I feel in the past few years that I've developed an ability to spot potential in others and have been able to foster their development. For me, that's the real challenge of leadership—helping others meet their potential.

Critique This response indicates that the applicant has a successful track record (adding an illustration would even strengthen it). More important, it shows that the applicant has an understanding of what the outcome of effective leadership can be, thus suggesting that he or she is speaking from experience.

QUESTION 31

In your adult life what accomplishment has given you the most satisfaction?

Analysis   The response to this question will give the interviewer a quick insight into your personal values and standards. What you choose to speak about will create an immediate impression of what you hold in high esteem.

Killer Answer   In my last job I managed to save enough money—from bonuses and some investments—to get the car of my dreams. I consider that a great accomplishment.

Critique   Aside from showing the candidate's ability to manage personal finances, this response does little to illustrate the candidate's maturity. On the contrary, by focusing on the fulfillment of a personal interest, the candidate shows a decided lack of emphasis on career aspirations.

Winner Answer   In my last job I took over my boss's responsibilities for two months while he was ill. Although I was relatively new to my own position, I was able to pick up the additional responsibilities and effectively meet the demands of both positions. It felt really satisfying to be able to respond to a crisis like that and deliver.

Critique   The strength of this response is that it relates a unique accomplishment, emphasizes the applicant's commitment and diligence, and suggests formidable competence. By addressing the nature of his or her satisfaction, the applicant paints a picture of a highly desirable candidate—one both willing and able to perform at an unusually high level.

QUESTION 32

What determines your personal choices, and would you agree that others should use that same criteria?

Analysis   One sign of maturity is to develop a way of making sense of the world. This question probes the extent to which a person has established a way of making choices that reflects his or her maturity.

Killer Answer   I like to take things as they come. I find that I can handle almost any situation if I have to. I don't really have a set of criteria; I just do what the situation demands. Besides, I don't think I can dictate to other people how they should handle things. I believe in everyone's individuality.

Critique   This response comes directly out of the "here and now, do your own thing" mentality of the 1960s and 1970s and will leave you at the unemployment office until the next fad comes and goes. To the potential employer this attitude reflects a lack of commitment and willingness to take a stand—both characteristics the employer of the 1990s wants dearly.

Winner Answer   It seems to me that the real challenge in today's fast-paced work world is maintaining a sense of balance. That way I'm sure to make choices that keep me feeling my best and most productive. I think a sense of balance is important for everyone interested in functioning at the highest level.

Critique   The most important thing about this response is that it shows that the applicant has thought about decision making and has developed an approach that works. In addition, the implication that the applicant can handle the demands of a highly competitive job is comforting to any employer taking on the responsibility of a potential employee's health care.

QUESTION 33

What would you do differently if you were to start college all over again?

Analysis   This question is designed to see if the applicant—particularly the recent graduate—has made the transition from student to adult in the way he or she thinks about learning.

Killer Answer   I don't think I'd change a thing. Those college years were wonderful years. Sometimes I wish I could replay them. You know I really got a lot out of school.

Critique   This response suggests that the applicant is still fighting adulthood, pining for the simpler, less responsible school days. It would send shivers up an interviewer's spine.

Winner Answer   I think if I were to start school all over again I would be less intimidated by the whole process. I would challenge my professors more; and I would use what I've learned about the system to make it work more to my advantage, to ensure that I got the most from the experience.

Critique   This response shows that the applicant has demystified the college experience and has developed a critical eye for analyzing experiences and systems. The response suggests that the applicant has high standards and is committed to high-quality learning.

QUESTION 34

What have been your greatest disappointments and how did you respond?

Analysis   Like the previous question, this one goes directly to the maturity issue. It reveals information about the applicant's standards, values, and priorities.

Killer Answer   When I first started working after I got out of school I was shocked at the expectations of most employers. The idea of spending 60 to 70 hours a week at work was a real shock. I believe that if you're really good you can do any job in no more than 45 to 50 hours a week.

Critique   Although the amount of time people are expected to work is an issue many professionals are now concerned about, the last thing an employer wants to hear is that you have specific restrictions on your time. In addition, choosing to respond to this question by complaining about employers' demands shows a decided lack of maturity.

Winner Answer   When I first got out of school I initially thought I would find a job and an organization that would last a lifetime. Once I got into the market I realized that finding the right job in the right company might take a while. Now that I understand the way the job market works a little better, I can handle it. The good jobs may take a little longer to find but in the long run I think it pays to be really careful.

Critique   This response shows that the applicant's priority is career stability. By emphasizing the quality of one's work situation as a key concern the applicant projects a sense of maturity and depth of understanding of the world of work. The response also suggests that the applicant can handle uncertainty—an important survival skill.

QUESTION 35

What are the most important rewards you expect from a job?

Analysis   Once again, what you choose to talk about directly reflects your level of maturity just as much as the position you take. Also important here is to remember the "no money talk" rule. Unless you're in negotiation, avoid talking about money.

Killer Answer   I want to work for an organization that recognizes quality and isn't afraid to reward a job well done. Since I expect to outperform my peers I would expect appropriate remuneration for my accomplishments.

Critique   Once again the problem of egos arises. In this response the person conveys a sense of inappropriate superiority and raises a red flag to the interviewer that says "difficult person."

Winner Answer   What's most important to me is that the job I take is a good match. By that I mean it will allow me to do what I do well—thus giving me a sense of satisfaction. I also want a job that demands that I stretch myself beyond my current level, forcing me to develop myself.

Critique   This double-barreled response—satisfaction from a job well done and the stretching of personal limits for growth—will leave the interviewer eating out of the palm of your hand.

QUESTION 36

Under what circumstances have your associates relied on you?

Analysis   One of the ways employers measure maturity is by assessing the extent to which an applicant demonstrates an ability to work with others. This question is targeted toward measuring the applicant's ability to engender trust from others and to work cooperatively.

Killer Answer   That happens all the time. Once people realize I'm good at what I do they rely on me to do it. That's really not a problem for me.

Critique   Note: Anytime someone says, "That's really not a problem for me," there's probably a problem. This is especially true in a case such as this, in which there was no suggestion that a problem might exist. The other problem with this response is that the answer is so vague and generalized that it lacks any sense of authenticity. The interviewer is left wondering if the applicant has a real problem with relationships or merely doesn't understand the importance of the question. In either case, a lack of depth or maturity would be the concern.

Winner Answer   I've often tried to look at the people I work with as a team. I think it makes sense in a competitive environment. Consequently I've often relied on co-workers and encouraged them to rely on me. One of the ways I try to do that is, for example, when I'm working on a particular project with someone else, I like to look at the strengths each of us brings to that project and then delineate roles based on our expertise. It usually works out pretty well.

Critique   This response suggests that the applicant knows how to create cooperative working relationships and has been successful in the past in gaining others' confidence. This response could be made even stronger by illustration—giving an example of an actual project in which the applicant created the sort of "expertise sharing" mentioned in the response.

QUESTION 37

What do you feel it takes to be a professional?

Analysis This question tells the interviewer how well the applicant is established in the working world. It also tells the interviewer the extent to which the applicant thinks of himself or herself as a serious, career-minded person rather than just another job hunter.

Killer Answer You've got to be really good at what you do. Once you achieve excellence in whatever it is you do and show it, then people treat you like a professional. I think it takes time and lots of work but eventually it's worth it.

Critique Here the interviewee presents a view of professionalism as something to be obtained, not something good employees (or prospective employees) already possess. By talking about other people's views (that is, being treated like a professional) the applicant suggests that professionalism is in the eye of the beholder—not in the actions of the employee.

Winner Answer To me, being a professional means that for any task I take on I do what needs to be done to achieve results. More than that it means taking responsibility for my own performance. Being a professional means most of all being my own taskmaster—in charge, you might say, of my own quality control.

Critique The greatest strength of this response is its language. By using such phrases as "achieve results," "responsibility for my own performance," and "my own quality control," the interviewee presents himself or herself as someone who delivers, needs little supervision, and understands the importance of self-motivation.

CATEGORY SIX: PLANNING AND ORGANIZING ABILITIES

In searching for strong candidates, organizational leaders know that they need people who can tolerate change and flux. The two key skills interviewers will be searching for in this section are the ability to plan and the ability to organize.

When seeking an understanding of a person's ability to plan, interviewers are looking for the applicant's understanding of the impact of the past on the present and the ability to use prior and current experience for creating plans for the future.

When seeking an understanding of an applicant's organizing ability, the interviewer is looking for an applicant's sense of order, sequence, and ability to see the whole picture.

This is a difficult category because the two areas of focus can be somewhat general. Therefore, it is important that the applicant's presentation be as specific and detailed as possible. When responding to questions about planning, responses that demonstrate one's planning skills in action are most effective. When responding to questions about organizing ability, responses presented in an organized, sequential manner are most effective.

QUESTION 38

How did you prepare for this interview?

Analysis   This question addresses the applicant's ability to plan by focusing on the one thing that the applicant and the interviewer have in common, the interview. It is an excellent opportunity to demonstrate one's ability to plan and organize information.

Killer Answer   Well, I really didn't have to plan much. You see I've been preparing myself to work in a high-powered company for a long time. This feels like a very natural move for me, so I just spent a little bit of time thinking about whether or not this was the right company for me and figured I'd give it a shot.

Critique   The real problem with this response, other than reflecting a lack of planning ability, is the assumption that the interviewer values spontaneity. What the applicant doesn't realize is that this question is a litmus test for the applicant's project management skills.

Winner Answer   The first thing I did was study your annual report. I then reviewed the major trade journals for articles on your company to see if there were any major projects going on that would shed light on the company. Then I called people I knew who had recently had some contact with you to find out what their impressions were. While doing all this I took some notes and reviewed them before coming in.

Critique   This response shows a clear, organized mind at work. It reflects the ability of the applicant to tackle a problem and generate the kind of data needed to move forward.

QUESTION 39

What are your personal long-term and short-term goals? How did you determine them? How on a long-term and short-term basis do you prepare to meet them?

Analysis This is a difficult question because it is really a four-part statement requiring a multitude of responses. Important to remember with this set of questions—and they are often presented as a set—is that you are being asked about personal goals, not professional ones. This is important because chances are you will be asked separately about professional aspirations, and if you don't distinguish the two you are left with the less than impressive choice of having to repeat yourself. Also important to note is that this question is in the planning and organizing section because it sheds light on your ability to use these skills in your personal life.

Killer Answer I read somewhere that my generation will be the first one in American history to be worse off than the previous generation. That concerns me and my goal is to make sure I don't come up short in the long run. That may sound pessimistic but I'm a realist and I believe it's important to face facts.

Critique Aside from focusing on the negative condition of the economy—an unwise move—this response is lacking for several reasons. First, it attempts to lump all the questions into one. Second, it is too "philosophical," thus revealing nothing about planning or organizing. Finally, it suggests that the applicant has a less than optimistic view of his or her future and is primarily concerned with overcoming obstacles and surviving— not thriving.

Winner Answer Like any realistic goals, mine change periodically. My personal strategy, both long- and short-term, is to assess continually where I am in relation to a current goal and modify plans as required. For example, every five years I establish a personal plan with an overall goal and set of objectives. I review my progress every six months and make the necessary modifications. My current plan obviously includes a career shift toward more satisfying work. Aside from that I'm meeting the personal goals I've set most recently.

Critique   This response shows an organized mind, one adept at planning. By discussing his or her approach to personal goal setting the applicant is able to convey a sense of self-esteem and confidence in his or her ability to manage personal affairs.

QUESTION 40

What is your personal and professional five-year goal?

Analysis   Like the previous question this one probes the ability to plan. In addition it lets the interviewer know the extent to which your goals match what the company can do for you.

Killer Answer   I like to play it one day at a time. With the way companies change hands today I think it's ridiculous to do too much personal planning, don't you?

Critique   This one belongs in the flake hall of fame. First, the popular ''one day at a time'' does not work when someone wants insight into your goals. Raising the undoubtedly uncomfortable notion that the company is vulnerable to raiders is also inappropriate. Finally, degrading the question by implying that planning is ridiculous and turning the question back to the interviewer would be the final nail in the coffin.

Winner Answer   Five years from now I'd like to have been in a good position for a few years, perhaps even have moved up once, and be looking for another step, either up or laterally within an organization. Personally, I'd like to think I could find an organization I could stay with for a while—one interested in making a mutual investment.

Critique   Without being overly specific (and possibly creating limits) this response shows the applicant to be ambitious and thoughtful about ways to get established in the organization. By talking about lateral shifts as well as upward moves, the applicant offers a view of himself or herself as a flexible candidate.

QUESTION 41

How would you go about creating a plan for your unit or department if you were in charge?

Analysis   This question is designed to discover directly the applicant's skill in organizational planning. The response will demonstrate the applicant's ability to take an open-ended situation and create a strategic plan.

Killer Answer   I guess I'd get everybody together, figure out what we needed to accomplish, set some goals and objectives, and then make it happen.

Critique   This answer suggests that the applicant knows little about strategic planning other than the need to set goals. It leaves the interviewer wondering if the applicant has the competence and confidence to lead.

Winner Answer   I believe that planning is one of the most critical skills a manager can have. The key is using a systematic process. First, you need to gather input from all staff members. Next you need to review and analyze the input. Once you understand what you're working with, you create a plan with goals and objectives. Next you implement the plan. Finally, you evaluate, on an ongoing basis, how things are going and adjust as required.

Critique   This response shows that the applicant is familiar and comfortable with the planning process. This systematic presentation of steps suggests that the applicant has done it before and is prepared to do it again.

QUESTION 42

What is your long-term occupational goal?

Analysis   The answer to this question will reveal a great deal about your attitude toward planning and your ability to think in a long-range way. Your response will give the interviewer insight into your method of planning. It will also provide information about your potential match with the organization.

Killer Answer   I think everybody's looking for the same thing. You want to be successful, move up the corporate ladder and eventually become head honcho. Of course if that's not possible at least become one of the key players.

Critique   Any impact this response might have is immediately diluted by suggesting that everybody wants the same thing. The response essentially says nothing about this person as an individual, except that he or she has blind ambition. Although there is an attempt in the end to back off, the damage is done, and the interviewer is left with a very vague impression of the applicant's plans.

Winner Answer   I'd like to think I could function in a leadership role in a solid organization. I've had a really strong track record so far, and I believe I've got what it takes to make a significant contribution. My aim is eventually to be responsible for large numbers of projects and people.

Critique   Although this response is somewhat open-ended it is specific enough to cor vey a sense of vision toward the future. The applicant uses the question as an opportunity to suggest that he or she has been a winner in the past and intends to continue in that pattern.

QUESTION 43

How important are details to you?

Analysis   This question will tell the interviewer how careful you are. It will reveal information about your sense of quality and your willingness and ability to do a thorough job.

Killer Answer   I think details are important when they influence the outcome of a situation. Sometimes, I think people spend too much time on details and it slows them down, preventing them from finishing their work, and that's unfortunate. I think some people don't know when to move on.

Critique   The biggest problem with this response is that it borders on complaint. The applicant is disparaging people who pay great attention to detail. What the applicant doesn't realize is that in a competitive environment it's often keen attention to detail that sets a company apart.

Winner Answer   I think that attention to detail can make the difference between acceptable results and excellent results. Building in quality controls from the start of a project is, I believe, a way to ensure that the project has the best possible outcome. I believe the more careful you are in the early stages of a project the less likely you are to have problems in the later stages.

Critique   This response assures the interviewer that the applicant appreciates the need for quality control. It also demonstrates an understanding of the planning process and shows that the applicant has done some thinking about, and perhaps had some success with, planning and organizing projects in the past.

QUESTION 44

How would you change your planning for your future course if you could?

Analysis This question will reveal the extent to which the applicant has insight into the consequences of planning. It will also tell the interviewer how well the applicant learns from past experience and applies that learning to new situations.

Killer Answer I wouldn't change a thing. Everything has gone so well for me that I'm sure if I keep using my best judgment I'll continue to be happy.

Critique This response shows a decided lack of insight and an inability to assess one's own actions critically. It also demonstrates a significant lack of depth in the applicant's understanding of the complexity of individual career development.

Winner Answer I think that when people are just starting their career they tend to assume they know what they want. If I could change anything it would be the care with which I made early decisions, like what to major in, summer jobs, early career decisions, that sort of thing.

Critique This response shows that the applicant has the ability to do some serious self-assessment. By acknowledging that some early decisions could have been handled differently, the applicant shows a willingness to learn from mistakes and critically assess and modify behavior to improve performance.

CATEGORY SEVEN: REACTION TO PRESSURE AND CHANGE

Ask about the stability of the contemporary U.S. corporation and those involved will tell you that one thing is constant— change. The ability to adapt to and thrive on change is considered a key characteristic of any applicant approaching the corporate arena. The demonstrated ability to respond effectively to pressure is a skill coveted by those choosing new employees for their organizations. Because of the constant pressure that comes with uncertainty, employers are increasingly looking for people who can function well when what's around the corner is a mystery. Your ability to respond positively to questions that shed light on your reactions to pressure and change will greatly enhance your chances. Remember that interviewers know that some people react to stress negatively and become paralyzed, whereas others react positively and become motivated. Being seen as someone who is motivated rather than paralyzed will take you far in the interview process.

QUESTION 45

If you were selling a product and you had a customer who was complaining about poor service, what would you do?

Analysis This question probes the applicant's ability to respond to and handle difficult people. The interviewer is looking for a response that suggests that the applicant is not easily intimidated.

Killer Answer I believe in the age-old adage, "The customer is always right." I would make sure that the customer left feeling fully satisfied with the product.

Critique Age-old is right! The interviewer probably heard this one from his or her grandfather. Don't insult interviewers by feeding them pap. Remember, the interviewer probably has an IQ equal to or greater than the applicant's.

Winner Answer I would explain that this company prides itself on quality goods and quality service. I would then assure the customer that I will do everything in my power to remedy the situation. Next, I would listen to the complaint, track the problem to its source, and make whatever changes are necessary to satisfy the customer.

Critique This response goes beyond the cliché of the Killer Answer and shows the applicant's true commitment to quality service. The response indicates that the applicant is not intimidated by problems and is willing to do what is necessary to resolve them.

QUESTION 46

What types of situations really get you down?

Analysis   This question is meant to discover your Achilles' heel. It will tell the interviewer what sorts of stress and pressure cause you to lose perspective, motivation, and performance ability.

Killer Answer   I don't get down too often. I'm pretty resilient. What slows me down is having to deal with other people's down times.

Critique   Although the respondent's instincts are right in not naming a true Achilles' heel (you never want to do that in an interview), denying any potential obstacles leaves the interviewer suspicious. The applicant also breaks the "don't put anyone else down" rule in this response, hinting at a weak character.

Winner Answer   I think the thing that bothers me most, and it doesn't happen often, is when a problem lingers too long. I don't think there's room in most successful organizations for unresolved problems. I like to find good solutions as quickly as possible so we can get on with the business of the organization.

Critique   This response offers a real answer but not a debilitating one. It gives the interviewer a reasonable response but doesn't cause worry about the applicant's abililty. It reassures the interviewer that the applicant is committed to both quality and timeliness.

QUESTION 47

What do you do when you know you're right and others disagree with you?

Analysis   This question probes an applicant's ability to work with opposing viewpoints and to tolerate the accompanying stress. It also probes the applicant's comfort and ability when handling conflict.

Killer Answer   First, I try to figure out a way to convince them that I'm right. If that doesn't work, and it usually does, I try to see if there's a way to work around their objections so they don't interfere with what I know to be the right approach.

Critique   Aside from smacking of egomania, this response has several additional problems. It implies that if the applicant cannot gain compliance from those with opposing viewpoints he or she will do what is necessary to have it the applicant's way. The response suggests a lack of ethical standards when faced with a difficult or conflict-laden situation.

Winner Answer   First, I make sure I have enough accurate information to maintain my position. Once I'm really convinced my perspective is the one to go with, I pay close attention to the particulars of the opposition's objections. I try to reason with them by looking at the situation from their perspective. Given mutual commitment I find agreement can eventually be reached.

Critique   This answer does several things. It shows that the applicant approaches conflict resolution from a problem-solving, win-win perspective. It shows that the applicant is open to change if that's what is called for. Finally it shows that the applicant takes a collaborative approach to solving difficult problems.

QUESTION 48

Do you feel qualified to be successful in your position, and if you don't, what will you do to compensate for your deficiencies?

Analysis Like the question that asks about weaknesses, this one should be handled carefully. To acknowledge that you have major shortcomings that would interfere with your work would merely serve to put you out of the running. If there are minor areas to work with, those might be mentioned, although unless your silence involves misinterpretation, it's better to wait until you're on the job to shore up the necessary areas.

Killer Answer This position is a piece of cake. I could do it with my eyes closed. I think if you hire me you'll be surprised at how quickly I'll be able to deliver for you. There isn't any part of this job I can't do.

Critique Although at face value this response may sound strong, the interviewee is guilty of overkill. In addition to arousing suspicion that there may be something beneath the surface, the applicant also creates doubt about the potential match. If the applicant is so extraordinarily capable of doing this job, perhaps the job is not enough of a challenge for that person.

Winner Answer Although I'm sure that there are things to learn—there are in every new job—I think you'll find that I'm a quick study. I've got the skills, and I believe the talent, to meet your needs and I don't see any real obstacles in my way.

Critique While acknowledging the need to learn some new things, the applicant presents confidence in his or her ability to do the job at hand.

QUESTION 49

Finish this sentence: Successful managers should. . . .

Analysis This question is designed to assess your potential for growth within the organization. Whether the job you are applying for has managerial responsibilities or not, your response will give the interviewer insight into your managerial potential—and insight into what it might be like being your manager.

Killer Answer To really stay on top of things I think a successful manager needs to know more about the work than the people being managed. That's the only way to maintain control over your employees—to know more than they do. Once you lose ground it's impossible to gain it back. You have to stay one step ahead of your troops.

Critique The first problem is that the applicant makes the managerial relationship sound like an adversarial one, not a cooperative one. The bigger problem, however, is suggesting that it is possible, let alone advisable, to know more than every employee in your charge about everything they do. Anyone at all in tune with the times and rate of change in technology, information dissemination, and organizational processes knows that this approach is impractical and self-defeating.

Winner Answer A successful manager needs to be able to analyze situations quickly, determine appropriate responses, and take action. Most important, though, I think, is a person's ability to read people. Each employee is unique. Knowing that and adapting your approach to one that will work each time is what successful management is all about.

Critique In very few words this response details the applicant's approach in a clear and confident way. It suggests that the applicant has a way of managing that works. Finally, the response suggests an understanding of how difficult management can be—a sentiment any manager is happy to hear.

QUESTION 50

How do you work under pressure?

Analysis   Perhaps obvious, this question is a direct approach to an applicant's response to pressure.

Killer Answer   I thrive on pressure. The more chaotic things get, the better I like it. After all, these days there's no success without pressure—it's a dog-eat-dog world. I have a much bigger problem with boredom. If there's nothing to do I can get lazy, but pressure, no problem.

Critique   This one falls into the "is this person for real" category. Aside from being unbelievable it has a negative tone and also suggests that without acute pressure the applicant would be unmotivated.

Winner Answer   Anyone who's doing work that's worthwhile will experience pressure on the job at times. I can handle a reasonable amount of pressure, and even extreme pressure when the circumstances demand it. The key to handling pressure for me is finding ways to manage situations to alleviate the intensity of the pressure—that way it doesn't interfere with my productivity. I know pressure comes with any job and I work well under pressure when it's necessary.

Critique   This response suggests that the applicant has realistic expectations about the nature and level of pressure on the job. The response is strong without being overly solicitous. The applicant presents a view of someone who has handled pressure in the past and has developed strategies for coping effectively with pressure on the job.

POWER PREP STRATEGY III

As said earlier, preparation is the linchpin of power interviewing. The following exercise will ensure that you are as prepared as possible for the most important questions likely to be asked.

The first part of this activity involves rating your level of preparation for each of the questions listed. The second part involves shoring up the answers that are not as strong as they could be.

First you will be asked to rate your preparation for each question on a scale of 1 to 5. A score of 5 means that you are totally prepared to respond to that question. A score of 1 means you are totally unprepared. A score of 3 means you are moderately prepared. When scoring yourself on each question consider both content and delivery as part of your preparation. For example, consider question 1: "Why do you feel you can be successful in this position?" If you know that you could be successful in this position and you know how to convey that belief, give yourself a rating of 5. However, if you feel confident about your ability to be successful in that position but are not sure how you would articulate that belief, give yourself a 3. If you're not sure about your potential for success and are unsure about how to convey your thoughts on it, give yourself a 1.

Each item that is rated 3 or under needs some attention if you are serious about having a power interview. If content is the problem, you need to spend some time searching your history (or your mind) to come up with a strong response. If delivery is the problem, you need to practice your responses to those key questions until you feel as confident as possible about them.

Review and rate each of the 50 questions by using the preceding criteria. Once you've finished the rating, transfer your scores to the coding sheet, noting which questions need content work and which delivery work. When you have finished, you will have a blueprint for what you need to do to strengthen your responses.

Category One: Aggressiveness and Enthusiasm

1. Why do you feel you can be successful in this
   position?   1 2 3 4 5

2. What is your greatest strength and weakness, and how will these affect your performance here? 1 2 3 4 5

3. Have you ever been put on the spot by a professor or advisor when you've felt unsure of yourself? How did you respond? 1 2 3 4 5

4. Have you ever received a grade lower than you expected? If so, what did you do about it? 1 2 3 4 5

5. For job advancement would you consider an advanced degree? 1 2 3 4 5

6. What competitive activities have you participated in? Were these worthwhile? 1 2 3 4 5

Category Two: Communication Skills

7. How do you go about influencing someone to accept your ideas? 1 2 3 4 5

8. What experience have you had in making oral presentations? How do you rate your skills in this area? 1 2 3 4 5

9. How would you compare your verbal skills to your writing skills? 1 2 3 4 5

10. What do you least like about writing a term paper? 1 2 3 4 5

11. How should supervisors and subordinates interact? 1 2 3 4 5

12. How would you be described by a close friend? 1 2 3 4 5

13. How do you get along with co-workers? 1 2 3 4 5

Category Three: Record of Success

14. What do you consider to be your most significant accomplishment and why? 1 2 3 4 5

15. Under what conditions have you been most successful in any undertaking?   1 2 3 4 5

16. How hard do you work to achieve your objectives?   1 2 3 4 5

17. Has competition had any positive or negative
impact on your accomplishments? How?   1 2 3 4 5

18. What do you consider your earning potential to
be five years from now?   1 2 3 4 5

Category Four: Rational Thought Process

19. What are the most important characteristics you
are looking for in a job and why?   1 2 3 4 5

20. How do you think our company determines
success?   1 2 3 4 5

21. What is the most intellectually challenging thing
you are looking for in a job and why?   1 2 3 4 5

22. What is the most intellectually challenging thing
you have ever done?   1 2 3 4 5

23. How did you determine your career choice?   1 2 3 4 5

24. What do you consider most valuable, a high
salary or job recognition and advancement?   1 2 3 4 5

25. Organize your ladder of success and explain this
progression.   1 2 3 4 5

26. What qualities are most important to determine
whom you would hire for this position?   1 2 3 4 5

27. What are some of the most creative things you
have done?   1 2 3 4 5

28. Do you agree that grade point average is an
indication of how successful you would be in
this company?   1 2 3 4 5

29. If you could construct your own job within our
organization, what factors would you include? 1 2 3 4 5

Category Five: Maturity

30. In what ways have you been a leader?　　　　　1　2　3　4　5

31. In your adult life what accomplishment has given you the most satisfaction?　　　　　　1　2　3　4　5

32. What determines your personal choices, and would you agree that others should use the same criteria?　　　　　　　　　　　　1　2　3　4　5

33. What would you do differently if you were to start college all over again?　　　　　　1　2　3　4　5

34. What have been your greatest disappointments and how did you respond?　　　　　　1　2　3　4　5

35. What are the most important rewards you expect from a job?　　　　　　　　　　1　2　3　4　5

36. Under what circumstances have your associates relied on you?　　　　　　　　　1　2　3　4　5

37. What do you feel it takes to be a professional?　　1　2　3　4　5

Category Six: Planning and Organizing Abilities

38. How did you prepare for this interview?　　　1　2　3　4　5

39. What are your personal long-term and short-term goals? How did you determine them? How on a long-term and short-term basis do you prepare to meet them?　　　　　　　1　2　3　4　5

40. What is your personal and professional five-year goal?　　　　　　　　　　　　1　2　3　4　5

41. How would you go about creating a plan for your unit or department if you were in charge?　　1　2　3　4　5

42. What is your long-term occupational goal?　　1　2　3　4　5

43. How important are details to you?　　　　　1　2　3　4　5

44. How would you change your planning for your future course if you could?　　　　　1　2　3　4　5

Category Seven: Reaction to Pressure and Change

45. If you were selling a product and you had a customer who was complaining about poor service, what would you do?   1 2 3 4 5

46. What types of situations really get you down?   1 2 3 4 5

47. What do you do when you know you're right and others disagree with you?   1 2 3 4 5

48. Do you feel qualified to be successful in your position, and if you don't, what will you do to compensate for your deficiencies?   1 2 3 4 5

49. Finish this sentence: Successful managers should. . . .   1 2 3 4 5

50. How do you work under pressure?   1 2 3 4 5

Coding Sheet

Code each of your scores for the 50 items in the following spaces. For each item on which you scored 4 or above, add a checkmark, indicating that you are prepared to respond strongly to that question. For each item on which you scored 3 or below, place a C next to those items for which you need more content and a D next to those for which you need to improve your delivery. Place a CD next to those items that need both more content and improved delivery.

1. __ 2. __ 3. __ 4. __ 5. __ 6. __ 7. __ 8. __ 9. __ 10. __

11. __ 12. __ 13. __ 14. __ 15. __ 16. __ 17. __ 18. __ 19. __ 20. __

21. __ 22. __ 23. __ 24. __ 25. __ 26. __ 27. __ 28. __ 29. __ 30. __

31. __ 32. __ 33. __ 34. __ 35. __ 36. __ 37. __ 38. __ 39. __ 40. __

41. __ 42. __ 43. __ 44. __ 45. __ 46. __ 47. __ 48. __ 49. __ 50. __

Once you've coded the 50 questions, use the coding sheet as your guide to fine-tuning your interview performance. Focus first on the items that need improvement both in content and in delivery, next focus on those items that need just content, and finally focus on those that need just a stronger delivery. Once you improve your performance on a question—you are the best judge—check that item off on the coding sheet. Once you've replaced all your letter codes with check-marks, you're finished!

There are many questions you can't anticipate in an interview—every situation is unique. The questions presented in this chapter are predictable. There's a good chance you'll get asked each of them in one form or another. Because all situations are different there will be times during the interview when you'll have to think on your feet. By preparing your responses to the 50 key questions you save your creative thinking energies for the unanticipated questions. The preparation you do with the questions in this chapter will allow you to enter the interview with confidence and the ability to perform far above the average applicant.

4

The Key Business Trends for the 1990s

Americans, and American businesses, love trends. Even more than trends, though, we are enamored of catchwords, words that conjure up images of success and prosperity. In the 1980s the word was *excellence*. Companies were committed to excellence, researchers were in search of excellence, and successful employees were purveyors of excellence.

While the concept of excellence, and its implications, still dominates the corporate landscape, it is losing ground in the career marketplace. Since the early 1980s when Peters and Waterman's *In Search of Excellence* became a best-seller, clever job applicants began quoting from the annals of "the excellence books" to woo their prospective employers. Although the principles of excellence are sound and make good sense to most forward-thinking organizational leaders, the word has lost its punch. Most interviewers have been so bombarded with it that the eyes glaze over when it is uttered. In fact, we heard of one business school professor who now forbids reference to any of "the excellence books" in his students' research papers because they had become so prevalent.

The astute job applicant would be wise to note the oversaturation of the term. Although it would be foolish and self-defeating to abandon the concept of excellence in the workplace, it makes sense to think of more original ways to articulate its virtues.

Prone toward trends and catchwords as we are, it would be a mistake to think that the "E" word will not be replaced in the 1990s by an equally brief, albeit potentially rich, word.

In fact, one word has begun to appear repeatedly. That word is *vision*. The word is not new, nor is its usage. In fact, "the excellence books" talked about vision. What is new is its pervasiveness, a presence and apparent dominance in the minds of those who run, watch, and write about businesses. Not coincidentally, many consulting firms that specialize in helping organizations create and articulate their visions have sprouted in recent years.

Having vision implies having foresight, a view of the future that determines the actions of the present. Vision is a picture in the mind's eye of a potential to be attained. When an organizational leader has vision, it means that he or she knows where the organization is going and what it is going to take to get there. When an employee has vision, it means that he or she has at least a commitment to an organization's future, and perhaps a handle on it.

High-technology companies have been fond of the word and the concept for some time. Apple Computer Company was founded and run in the early 1980s on the vision of its co-founder Steve Jobs. Although that vision eventually ran aground, the concept and its power are still revered. When Digital Equipment Corporation built its "experimental" plant in Enfield, Connecticut, it named the street on which it stands Vision Drive.

When corporate leaders talk about the transformation of their companies, transformations increasingly common in this age of mergers, buyouts, and retrenching, they invariably discuss their vision as the driving force for the company.

You may be wondering what all this has to do with your job hunt. While you obviously can't be the visionary for an organization you are not yet a part of, there are several ways this notion of vision can help you.

First, since the concept itself is popular, it can help you if you talk about the importance of vision for the organization and the individual. Current corporate lore suggests that if the organization does not have a vision to propel it, it is going nowhere. Similarly, the individual lacking vision is headed for a comparable fate. More important, understanding and appreciating the vision of the leaders of an organization you are courting can provide great opportunity in an interview.

For example, if you were interviewing with IBM, and you knew that CEO John Akers's vision for the future was to make his company "the world's champion in meeting the needs of the customer," imagine the headway you could make. Showing the interviewer what you have to offer that contributes to meeting the needs of the customer would undoubtedly make a favorable impression. In addition, conveying an appreciation for the CEO's vision of customer service would enhance the likelihood of your being seen as a potential corporate match.

Finally, since vision is "in," it is quite possible that you might be asked in an interview to articulate a vision of yourself working in the position for which you are applying. You should be prepared to respond with an answer that shows your appreciation of the value and importance of having and sustaining vision.

In this chapter you will be briefed on 12 key business trends for the 1990s. Incorporate these trends into your own vision and adapt them to what you know about the thrust of the particular company to which you are applying. Chances are your vision will overlap with the vision of the leaders of the organization, and more important, with the vision of your interviewers.

TREND ONE

Global Competition

Unless you've had your head in the sand you know that America's most successful companies have been facing stiff competition from all over the world, particularly the Far East. The elimination of trade barriers in Europe as of 1992 will mean increased competition from that part of the world as well. The competition faced by the U.S. corporation means that in order to survive and thrive into the next century, companies and the people who work in them must become "globally comfortable." This does not mean you need to speak German and Japanese (although that wouldn't hurt). What it does mean is that you need to have a global perspective and that you somehow need to convey that perspective in the interview. Essentially, you need to show the interviewer that you understand and appreciate the fact that what happens in the world has an impact on your company and that what happens in your company could have an impact on the world.

In addition you need to let your prospective employer know that you are willing to travel abroad if your work demands it. In fact, most observers of life in corporate America believe that the typical CEO of the future will most likely have had some experience overseas. In a 1987 report on the economy of the 1990s, *Fortune* magazine predicted a 280 percent rise in the export of U.S. services, including banking, accounting, engineering, management consulting, data processing, advertising, and law. Cited as the reasons for this growth were U.S. service industries' advantages in scale, market reach, capital depth, and technological prowess.

The extent to which you can demonstrate your understanding that the world in fact has become "a global village" will greatly influence your chances in the corporate marketplace. The extent to which you can demonstrate your willingness and ability to adapt and respond to life in the global village will have an impact on your desirability. The more knowledgeable you are about other countries and the ways they work, and the more comfortable you are working with them, the more desirable you will be.

So pervasive is the notion of global competition that some observers believe that in the future corporate lines of demarcation will replace national ones. The Singer sewing machine is an example of shifting boundaries. The shell is made in Cleveland, the motor in Brazil, the drive shaft in Italy—and it is assembled in Taiwan. Recent movements toward democratization in places like East Germany and Poland suggest that the homogenization of the world and the notion of corporations replacing countries may not be as farfetched as it may seem. Although we're still probably a few decades away from corporate states instead of nation states, there is no doubt that any product or service of significance produced and marketed in America will face competition from abroad. Your understanding of global complexity and your willingness to engage in global competition will set you strides above applicants who think only locally and nationally.

TREND TWO

The Flattening of Organizational Frameworks

Tell a corporate recruiter that your professional goal is to move up the organizational hierarchy and you'll probably get laughed out of the room. In the company of the 1990s the hierarchies are giving way to flatter organizational structures that require managers and other employees to take on increasingly more responsibility with decidedly less authority. There are more people being asked to take on roles that involve wearing many hats and fewer people sitting at the top of the hierarchy watching the others do the work. The U.S. company of the 1990s is the hands-on company. Recruiters don't want to hear your lofty goals about someday being the head of a division. They want to hear about your willingness and ability to work as part of a team, to solve problems, and to make things happen. The more willing you are to start at the bottom and work your way up—or work your way in—the better. Corporations are inundated with new MBAs wanting to start at high-level positions. While the MBA remains a valuable credential for entry into the better companies, an attitude that it gives you special privileges is dangerous. Today's leading companies want applicants who know that career ladders are splintering and being replaced by bridges that can lead to more valued positions in the organization. Many good jobs are available to those willing to pay their dues in exchange for ownership (either actual or symbolic) in the company. The key is showing that you understand the way things are and that you are willing to participate.

The hierarchy is being replaced by the network. Consequently, organizations are looking for people who are able to manage relationships up, down, and across departmental and division lines. High-potential employees will be those who are comfortable as network managers rather than those concerned only with pleasing those above them. A profile of corporate giant U.S. West illustrates this point. A recent article in *U.S. West Today* described the ideal candidate as someone who is neither a specialist nor a generalist, but what is called ''a totalist.'' A totalist is someone who is a sort of Renaissance employee. That person knows a lot about one area, and a bit about the rest of the company's areas, and is comfortable moving freely from one thing to another. An ability to manage relationships across division lines and throughout the shrinking hierarchy is considered a vital skill, as is an ability to perform a wide variety of tasks.

Demonstrating an understanding of the shift from hierarchies to flatter organizational structures will convey to your interviewer that you have an up-to-date understanding of contemporary organizational life and its demands.

TREND THREE

Managing Diversity

All the demographic indicators suggest that the core of the U.S. work force is dramatically changing. The days when white males made up a company's entire roster of employees are over. Increasingly organizations will be staffed and run by women and people of color. (The term "people of color" refers to all people who do not fit the category "white" and is used to ensure that people of all cultural backgrounds are included in the discussion.) Whether you are a white male, a woman, or a person of color, the extent to which you are comfortable working with people from diverse backgrounds will dramatically affect your chances and your success. Gaining familiarity and feeling comfortable working with people from different cultural and gender backgrounds will help you to negotiate your way into positions and to be successful there.

Managing diversity involves more than expressing a belief in women's rights or in equal opportunity for all. It involves a commitment to understanding the ways in which people different from yourself operate. It involves an understanding of the ways people from other cultures communicate and negotiate in the world around them. The classic example often sited in classes on cultural diversity (classes well worth taking) is the case of the Hispanic child who is repeatedly reprimanded by the white teacher for being disrespectful for not looking the teacher in the eye while being scolded. What the white teacher does not know is that looking down when being spoken to by an adult is a sign of respect in that child's world. Consequently, the teacher's ignorance of cultural difference perpetuates the problem.

There are many subtle and some not so subtle cultural differences operating in an increasingly diverse work force. The first step in improving your ability to manage diversity is to become aware of your own behavior and its cultural bias. One vivid example of cultural bias at work comes from a piece of research conducted by three sociologists, Carol Word, Mark Zanna, and Joel Cooper, reported in a 1974 issue of the *Journal of Experimental Social Psychology.* In the experiment white job interviewers interviewed both black and white applicants. Through observation in a one-way mirror, the researchers observed that the white interviewers treated the black interviewees differently than the white interviewees by placing their chairs farther apart, making less eye contact, sitting in a less direct position, and ending the interview significantly sooner. When debriefed on the interview, most of the subjects were unaware of the subtle differences with which they treated the two groups of interviewees. Most experts agree that the first step in improving your ability to manage diversity is to gain a better understanding of your own bias, both conscious and subconscious, and overcome those aspects of your own behavior that could lead to unfair treatment.

In addition, understanding how people from various backgrounds operate can enhance your ability to perform on the job. As in the example of the Hispanic student and the white teacher, a lack of understanding can lead in many ways to misunderstanding and inappropriate responses in the workplace. For example, one of the cultural groups gaining prominence in the past ten years in this country is the Japanese. Anyone who thinks that understanding the Japanese is not important to U.S. business would seem, to any savvy businessperson, to be quite out of touch. At last count the Japanese owned four of the five biggest banks in the world and a good portion of the commercial real estate in almost every major U.S. city, including New York. If you are in any major business, from cars to computers, you are likely to run into a chief Japanese competitor. You also may find yourself working for the Japanese, as did everyone at Columbia Records when Sony Corporation recently bought it. In the 1974 book *Foundations of Intercultural Communication*, authors Sitaram and Cogdell reported on some of the differences between Asian styles of communicating and white American styles. Some ways in which people with Asian backgrounds might communicate differently than white Americans are using tradition to support an argument, focusing on group welfare versus the individual, avoiding direct criticism, and valuing silence in conversation.

Perhaps even more important to managing diversity than

understanding foreign competition is understanding the groups likely to provide large segments of the U.S. work force in the 1990s. The Department of Labor recently reported that the number of black Americans in the work force increased from approximately 8 million in 1965 to 12.4 million in 1985; and the number of Hispanic workers nearly doubled between 1975 and 1985, to 7.7 million from 4.2 million. The estimates indicate that during the 1990s nonwhites will account for one-third of all new workers. Some estimates suggest that only 15 percent of the new entrants to the work force will be white males. These figures suggest that blacks, Hispanics, and Asians will make up a significant number of the U.S. work force. If you are a member of one of these groups, the challenge is to establish your value in what can often prove to be a hostile environment. If you are white, the challenge is to heighten your own awareness and find ways to communicate and co-exist with this increasingly diverse work force. The extent to which you can communicate an ability to understand and work with a diverse work force will influence your ability to persuade prospective employers that you are someone capable of helping their company thrive in the inevitable diversity of the 1990s.

Understanding and Using Computers

As computers and computer networks become more sophisticated, people working in the companies for whom those systems are designed need to become highly proficient in their use. If you're uncomfortable with computers or unfamiliar with their use you'd better get over that or start looking elsewhere for work (perhaps in some other century). The computer revolution is as much a part of contemporary life in corporate America as the business suit or the telephone. Many jobs once performed by people, or currently performed by people, will be taken care of in the future by a network of computers. Your job will be to manage the use of the computers effectively, and to find better ways to utilize them, regardless of your work. The extent to which you can demonstrate an understanding and mastery of computer technology, the more likely you will be seen as a potentially valuable player.

Just as it is difficult to find a middle-class American home that does not have a VCR, it will be difficult to find an executive team in the 1990s that does not rely on computers. Computer technology is moving so fast that those not committed to keeping up will be left in the dust. For example, a new advancement in computer application is decision technology. In one of its applications, collections of computers and databases, called executive information systems, provide instant in-depth information on every aspect of a company for strategic planning and corporate decision making. While some CEOs are shying away from this technology because they fear it stifles their creativity, many are embracing it, acknowledging the power it has to make their decisions more prudent. Three new tools have emerged through the use of the microcomputer to help managers think more clearly about their businesses. One, cognitive mapping is used when decision makers are unclear about what decisions need to be made. It is essentially a brainstorming tool to help clarify what needs to be done. Two, decision mapping helps decision makers consider the impact of a decision on a wide range of organizational variables. Three, microworld technology constructs a simulated model of an organization to help users consider a broad range of organizational moves. Although each of these concepts existed before the widespread use of the microcomputer, they are enjoying increased popularity as they become simplified and more usable.

Without getting too complicated, it is easy to see that without a basic knowledge and appreciation of computer technology and a willingness to stay abreast of new developments, one could easily be left behind. The serious contender in any power interview would be wise to develop an up-to-date knowledge of computer applications and their potential impact on any target organization.

TREND FIVE

Teams, Teams, Teams

Anywhere you go in corporate America today you hear talk of teams. All the buzz about participatory management has made way for the teamwork revolution. By all indicators, the manager of the past who orders underlings around will be replaced by the orchestrator, the leader who effectively creates, monitors, and assists groups of people working together to get the job done. Your success as a member of a team will be determined by your ability to work cooperatively with other team members toward a given end. Your success as a potential organizational leader will be determined by your capacity to empower others, instill a sense of commitment, and help articulate a team vision that reflects the broader organizational vision. Your ability to couch your skills in terms that suggest you have what it takes to work successfully in and manage teams will greatly enhance your chances of getting the highly sought-after jobs.

The concept of teamwork in the workplace was initially an American idea. However, ironically it was not implemented here and has not been taken seriously until recent years. After World War II, however, the Japanese, determined to rebuild their economy—and comfortable with the notion of teamwork because of their cultural emphasis on the group rather than on the individual—embraced the idea wholeheartedly. In fact, some analysts suggest that the Japanese comfort with team-work is to some extent responsible for their current prominence in the world market.

In recent years U.S. corporations have made attempts to emulate their Japanese counterparts with the introduction of quality circles—groups that attempt to solve organizational problems by holding brainstorming sessions; employee in-volvement programs; and a decidedly American twist on the concept, employee stock ownership plans. A prime example of such efforts is a joint project of General Motors and Toyota in Freemont, California, where Japanese-style team management has been extraordinarily successful.

Productive and profitable as it may seem, teamwork in the

U.S. workplace is struggling. Americans, it seems, are decidedly individualistic and have trouble, by many accounts, in making teamwork work. In fact, most companies report less than favorable results from their efforts to switch from a traditional approach to a team approach. In spite of its failings, however, team management is considered to be, by many accounts, the wave of the future in the United States. In 1987, the U.S. General Accounting Office found that 70 percent of 476 large companies were using the simplest form of teamwork, quality circles. Boeing, Caterpillar, Ford, General Electric, General Motors, and Digital Equipment Corporation are only a few of the major companies that strongly espouse the teamwork concept. In the past teamwork strategies and talk of cooperation were met with resistance by middle managers, fearful of losing their roles, and by union leaders, fearful of losing their power. However, recent threats to their security by foreign competitors who use teams freely have gradually changed the attitudes of many opponents of participation. A recent convention of the United Auto Workers, in which workers voted by a large majority for employee involvement, signals that worker participation and teamwork are here to stay.

Although you don't need to be an expert in the technology of employee involvement, you do need to have an understanding of the basics and be prepared to present yourself as a team player with strong team management skills. Many organizational leaders are looking for people who are comfortable with the team concept and have some understanding of how it works. The more you know about teamwork and the various forms it can take, the more attractive you will be to an increasing number of organizations committed to this concept.

TREND SIX

The Service Obsession

If U.S. corporations pay attention to demographic trends, and they do, they know that what will separate the winning companies of the 1990s from the losing ones is service. In various segments of the population, consumers are screaming for service. Dual-career couples with young children want quality service. The huge mass of people entering their "golden years" demand service. Ken Dychtwald, CEO of Agewave and an expert on the needs and interests of aging America, spends a good deal of his time consulting with companies on how to modify products to meet the needs of older consumers. For example, one of his suggestions to the Avis car rental company was to provide a special service to customers over a certain age, such as a car at the airport door with their luggage already in the trunk. It's service like that, suggests Dychtwald, that the public wants—and will pay for. Demographers tell us that it is these two segments of the population, the baby boomers and the aged, that make up the lion's share of the buying public— and they're the ones with the most money to spend. If you want a job with a leading company, you'd better know this, and you'd better let your prospective employer know that you are committed to quality service because you recognize it as a key to organizational prosperity.

Service comes in many forms. Most of us can readily think of times when we've had inferior service. It's much harder to think of an incident of extraordinarily good service. Marketing experts tell us that one of the key variables determining customer loyalty is the experience the customer has during the transaction. Even industries whose primary competitive edge is the service they supply seemingly wear blinders when it comes time to make service-minded decisions. The shift in the 1980s to automated tellers in banks is a good example. While customers find them handy during off-hours, research suggests that given the option, a customer would prefer to interact with another person—not a machine. In many banks, the shift to automated tellers at the teller cages resulted in a loss of customers.

When I was shopping for stereo equipment recently I was more careful than usual. I had recently been burned by an inexpensive tape deck that warbled almost from the day I bought it. When I brought it in for repair I was told, as I was handed the bill, that there was nothing wrong with it; it just needed a cleaning. I brought it home only to find the warble unchanged. This time I went to a shop that was new in the area but was developing a reputation for high-quality service. During my conversation with the salesperson I was told that the shop had made a commitment to outstanding service—and that to date it had not charged any customer for a single repair and hoped to continue the policy as long as possible. The salesperson got my attention and my business.

Service is intangible and therefore sometimes illusive. Yet it is clear that the United States has suffered a crisis in service in recent years and that a key to a company's prosperity will be to make people feel good about how they purchased something as well as what it is they purchased.

As we move to more of a service economy it becomes evident that without attention to service no company will survive and thrive. Whether you're approaching a hardware store for the best way to winterize your house or a clever salesperson to help you pick out your next interview outfit, chances are you will buy at—and come back to— the place that gave you the best and most informed service.

For example, one of the industries to blossom in the midst of America's service-obsessed consumerism is the overnight mail business. The successful companies in this business base their success on providing timely, efficient, and effective service. Federal Express, one of the giants in the field, knows that its success is no accident. It has an extensive service-training program for all new employees. Anyone in the company who has contact with customers receives two to five weeks of customer-service training and follow-up training later on.

Since service will be the life blood of any organization in both the near and distant future, it makes sense for you to develop a keen appreciation for it. You would also be wise, when interviewing with any organization, to think about ways in which high-quality service manifests itself in that organization and to let your interviewer know of your sensitivity to it.

TREND SEVEN

From Brawn to Brains

Whereas it's always been true that the best companies rely on a pool of highly intelligent and resourceful people to run their organizations, the intelligence factor has become increasingly important. There was a time when working harder could deliver. That is no longer true. Companies are more than ever looking for people who work smarter. It is the belief of many in corporate America that intellectual capital rather than physical capital will be the driving force behind the successful companies. People who can manage information well will be the stars. Demonstrating an understanding of organizational systems in all their forms; of telecommunications; and as mentioned earlier, of computers, both hardware and software, will set the smart applicant apart from the crowd.

In particular an understanding of and adeptness at creating software will be extremely valuable. Knowing how to encode knowledge, to convey information through software, will be a skill highly valued in the techno-workplace of the 1990s.

But software is merely a vehicle for an information society. What is perhaps most striking about the changes in the business world is the enormity of the change. Consider this observation from an Associated Press article of July 23, 1989, by Peter Coy: "In 1866 international communication was only for the elite. It cost one hundred dollars to send a twenty-word cable from New York to London on the first undersea cable. Today it costs one dollar to send about four thousand words over the same route using an ordinary personal computer and modem." The information float has indeed collapsed, and the flood of knowledge in and out of organizations is more intense than ever.

The key to global competitiveness is knowledge. Gaining and using information more quickly and more effectively will be vital to a company's prosperity. Job applicants who demonstrate an understanding of the importance of knowledge and the ability to gather, process, and use information will be worth a great deal.

Because of the information explosion, education and training have become a side industry of many companies. IBM spends $900 million dollars a year on education and training. Aetna Insurance Company's Aetna Institute for Corporate Education has an operating budget larger than that of many colleges. Why is there such a commitment to education and training? Companies realize that without the brainpower they will be left in the dust. For example, most managers of engineering believe that without constant upgrading, the typical engineer's knowledge base would be totally obsolete within three years.

Showing an appreciation for the nature of the knowledge explosion and a commitment and ability to remain up to date in your personal knowledge base will take you far in the information age and in the power interview.

TREND EIGHT

Quality Is Job One

This by now familiar quotation—Quality is job one—by one of America's leading auto makers reflects a growing concern in the corporate world. Management guru Tom Peters caught the attention of the U.S. automobile industry when he decried the inferiority of his GM truck, talking about "minor" problems like a failed fourwheel drive light and a rattling glove compartment lock. Peters's popularity and his widespread appeal sent a message to the industry that he—and the American consumer— would not tolerate poor quality. The mythology around quality seems directly related to the prosperity of a company. For example, there's a story about a Honda employee, who, on his way home from the factory, would stop and adjust the windshield wiper blades on any Hondas he passed to ensure that they were "just right." The contrast between Peters's story about his GM truck and the Japanese employee's attention to detail paints a disturbing impression of the two competitors' attention to quality.

Increasingly, U.S. companies are becoming concerned about producing high-quality products. Quality control is considered a major concern in most companies, and corporate leaders are looking for people who know how to create conditions that foster a commitment to high quality that is organization-wide. So adamant about quality and its impact is management seer Peters that in his book, *Thriving on Chaos* (p. 72), he gives the following example: "A brochure is going out to customers. You've already missed your deadline. Five thousand have been printed, inserted into envelopes, addressed and sealed, and are packed and ready to be taken to the post office. Your small unit's cash flow is pinkish to red in hue. And then you discover a single typo on page two, in the small print. Should you walk past it or act? Easy. Act—throw it out!"

Now you might think that this tactic is a bit overzealous, but it points out how adamant people are becoming about quality. This is not just Peters's view but rather a view that he reports is held by many of the most successful companies in America—

large and small. Even if you think Peters takes the emphasis on quality too far, the important thing to note is that being a zealot for quality can only help your chances in any forward-thinking company. In fact, one of the key concerns for many organizational leaders is finding ways to build in commitment to quality and develop strategies for motivating employees toward producing consistently high-quality products. If you really want to gain points with your interviewers, show them you have ideas about ways to ensure quality in your work and to foster quality in the work of those around you.

Quality assurance, the buzzword for programs and departments that work on improving quality, has established itself so firmly in corporate America that it has even become a potential career path for some workers. Peters reports on one welder who became so involved in quality control that he was asked to make a presentation on quality at a company-sponsored Japanese Management Association Meeting; eventually he became a supervisor and an articulate spokesperson for quality throughout the company.

One thing is certain about the companies that survive and thrive through the 1990s: Quality will make the difference. Most competitive companies are keenly aware of the fact that a major reason the Far East has so successfully infiltrated the U.S. marketplace is simply that the products produced have often been of better quality than comparable U.S. products. An applicant's understanding of and commitment to quality will assure the interviewer that the applicant has an appreciation of the competitive marketplace that will help keep the company on top.

TREND NINE

The Human Side

Companies are showing an unprecedented concern for employees, being more sensitive about child care, parental care, employee assistance, and health care. All indications are that employees will continue to find their organizations increasingly responsive to their needs. Lest the reader, or the job applicant, think that a wave of altruism is spreading through the land, consider the wise words of *Megatrends* author, John Naisbitt. Naisbitt says that social change occurs in America only when economic necessity dictates. If organizations will be treating people better, one explanation is that they must do so in order to survive. Several factors suggest that this might be true. First is the impending labor shortage. Most demographic indicators suggest that in the 1990s there will be a shortage of qualified people to fill crucial jobs in many organizations. This impending shortage means that if you've got good employees, you had better keep them. The other explanation also has to do with demographic factors but with a little different slant. With the flattening hierarchies and emphasis on teams discussed earlier, organizations will need fewer middle managers. With fewer opportunities for advancement, organizations are faced with the problem of finding other ways to keep employees. One strategy, being used by an increasing number of organizations, is a developmental model that looks at employee growth as a means of retention. By getting to know employees better as people, management can find out what their needs and interests are and how it can provide incentives other than promotions to keep them happy.

With all these changes comes the reality that the successful organizations will be the ones that are able to hang on to valuable people. By showing your prospective employer that you have an understanding of human motivation and know how to keep other employees happy, you present yourself as someone who could be a potential solution to a looming problem of employee shortages.

One interesting development in the 1980s has been the embracing of the human potential movement by business. The human potential movement, developed in the early 1960s by psychologists, philosophers, and various other practitioners, concerns itself with stretching the boundaries of human consciousness by experimenting with alternative ways of being. In the 1970s the movement continued to develop momentum, but it wasn't until the 1980s that it became a part of mainstream America. Some observers attribute its acceptance, once again, to demographic factors, suggesting that the children of the 1960s will be the corporate leaders of the 1990s and that they're bringing their values with them. Others argue that it is older, wiser leaders who are bringing human potential into the workplace. Whatever the causes it is clear that wherever you look in business today, leaders are articulating the need to take care of people. All the best-selling management books—books written by and about the leadership of corporate America—place attention to people as a first priority. In his recent book, *Leadership Is an Art*, Herman Miller Furniture Chairman Max Depree talked about the role of an organizational leader as being one that enables and empowers people. Leaders, he maintained, need to create environments that foster the development of high-quality relationships between individuals, among work group members, and between employees and clients and customers. Depree's beliefs about what it takes to be successful in corporate America are being echoed throughout every forward-thinking company, both large and small.

As an interviewee you can be sure that whatever position you're seeking, those on the other side of the fence will be looking for someone who is sensitive to the needs of people. Present yourself as someone who appreciates the relationship between good people skills and the bottom line and you will make great headway in your search.

TREND TEN

Value-Added

Downsizing has had and will continue to have a major impact on the work force of the future. With the "fat trimmed" it becomes essential that the lean organization be one where every player makes a significant contribution. The increasingly popular term *value-added* reflects this mentality. Value-added means that everyone in the company will be able to demonstrate in very specific terms the impact of his or her contribution on the strength and prosperity of the organization. The growing belief that a key to any company's success is the ability for the leaders and employees to utilize each other to the maximum so that each player makes a clear measurable contribution is the core of the value-added mentality. The value-added concept is an outgrowth of the accountability movement of the 1970s and early 1980s and has been spurred on by economic hardships. The result is a reshuffling of what gets done in many organizations and by whom. The value-added movement has in fact restructured many industries and spawned some new ones. For example, during the 1960s and 1970s many companies developed large human resource departments where they employed what were called internal consultants to help with management development, training, and other human resource functions. With the value-added movement came questions about the contribution of these functions to the bottom line or the added value of the organization. Since these functions could not be tied directly to the bottom line they were considered "soft" and in many cases were eliminated or scaled back.

What has emerged to replace these internal roles are consulting firms whose purpose is to provide human resource functions to companies who need them. In the human resource company, the human resource function is a value-added function since it is the product or service that the company provides. Thus what has occurred is the elimination of certain roles and the emergence of companies whose primary role is the performance of those eliminated internal functions.

When approaching an organization you need to be keenly aware of the value-added mentality, which is predominating in most contemporary organizations. You need to present a case for joining the organization that highlights what your value-added contribution would be. In fact, recent advice on the part of many recruiters to people seeking to work in organizations where there is no specific opening is to gain entry into the organization through the sales department. If you want to get your foot in the door, they say, start out in sales, where the value-added connection is most obvious. Remember, in an increasingly competitive world, the bottom line, more than ever, is the bottom line.

TREND ELEVEN

Keep It Clean—Ethics in the Workplace

A few years ago a cartoon was widely circulated on many university campuses in which a student was trying to sign up for a course on business ethics. The caption read, ''Make up your mind: Which is it, business or ethics?'' That cartoon is no longer relevant. Today, a business student would be hard pressed to find a program in which business ethics was not at least an elective and most likely a requirement.

These days there is much talk of ethics in corporate hallways. Recent scandals on Wall Street and the failure of some large corporations to meet their moral obligations have left an impression of deteriorating conditions. Increased intolerance by the public regarding environmental abuse and financial misconduct has sent a message that the leaders of many companies are heeding. Those perpetuating or willing to tolerate unethical behavior in their organizations are seeing the impact that consumer boycotts and bad press can have. The applicant aware of the new ethical standards spreading through the corporate sector would be wise to communicate an appreciation of those standards during the selection process.

More than a minimal level of ethics will be required in the organization of the 1990s. Because of such organizational changes as shrinking numbers of employees, management-labor alliances, employee involvement, global joint ventures, and quality improvement programs, organizations will need unprecedented levels of trust and integrity in the work force. Although fierce competition is not likely to disappear, organizational leaders will also be concerned with creating alliances within and between companies that result in win-win situations. This changing mentality will create a job market in which high moral and ethical standards in applicants will be highly prized.

The interesting thing about ethics is that you can't see it, taste it, feel it, or hear it, yet each of us has our own sense of it. Like fingerprints, your ethics are unique—and you leave them everywhere you go. No one compromises or changes your ethics but you. Ethics cannot be prescribed, nor can they be feigned. Developing a strong sense of ethics can protect you in the marketplace. No job, promotion, or amount of money is worth a compromise of your ethics. Solid companies know this and will respect a person with high ethical standards.

Developing and living by a high level of ethical standards makes good sense for you as a person and as a professional. Communicating a high level of moral and ethical standards in an interview will help you find the best jobs in the best places— where ethics count.

TREND TWELVE

Risky Business

The shift toward greater accountability should not be confused with the notion of playing it safe. With the onset of global competition, the information explosion, and the emphasis on creativity and innovation, U.S. companies are looking for people who are not afraid to take risks. The ability and the willingness to take shrewd yet calculated risks is an important attribute for anyone seeking power positions in the contemporary organization.

In a recent speech to MBA candidates at the University of Pennsylvania's Wharton School, Raymond W. Smith of Bell Atlantic Corporation said, ''Don't make the mistake of confusing what a big company will tolerate with what it rewards. . . . Taking the safe road, doing your job, and not making waves may not get you fired (right away at least), but it sure won't do much for your career or your company over the long haul. We're not dumb. We know that administrators are easy to find and cheap to keep. Leaders—risk takers—are in very short supply. And ones with vision are pure gold.''

The key to remaining competitive in the global market, by most accounts, is to develop and foster know-how and inventiveness—to try new things. Companies concerned with holding their own and increasing their market share want people who are visionaries, people not afraid to find a new angle on an old problem.

While applicants who convey an ability to manage a unit effectively may get some of the jobs, those with the best chances will be the ones who convey an ability to lead others into an ambiguous and volatile future.

In the battle for market niches in the 1990s innovation and risk taking will determine the winners and losers. One vivid example of the potential for great loss or gain is the electronics industry. American manufacturers lost an enormous market niche in VCRs by not fine-tuning their machines as quickly as did their Japanese counterparts. Consequently, not a single VCR is manufactured in the United States today. High-definition television (HDTV) is in a similar position to that of the VCR ten years ago. Most observers in the industry believe that the key to conquering that potentially enormous market will be the extent to which U.S. companies can harness their creativity, move forward with innovative designs, and take the risks required to launch such a massive endeavor.

Risk taking in the contemporary company is fueled by accepting and embracing creativity in the workplace. Until recently creativity was regarded as something a limited number of people possessed. People considered creative would most often be found in research and development or in marketing. As companies seek new ways to compete and thrive in the marketplace, organizational leaders are looking for people who can find creative solutions to a broad range of organizational problems. From shortening production processes to naming products to eliminating the need for stock rooms (it's called on-time production), companies are relying on creative ways to cut costs and improve productivity. Not only have creativity and the risk taking it has spawned become acceptable in the contemporary workplace, but they are also coveted.

An applicant's ability to convey a sense of adventure, a knack for creative thinking, and a willingness to take risks will not go unnoticed in the forward-thinking company of the 1990s.

POWER PREP STRATEGY IV

This chapter presented a primer on the key trends for the 1990s. You can be sure, given the volatility of the world economy and the struggle for U.S. companies to redefine themselves, that these trends are on the minds of corporate leaders everywhere. Interviewers will be looking for applicants who understand these trends and appreciate their significance. Power Prep Strategy IV will help you identify those trends that you are familiar and comfortable with and those that need further attention. For the answers to some of the questions you may have to refer back to the text; for others, you may have to do some research on the company; and for some, you'll have to search your own background. Complete the following questionnaire on the 12 trends and you'll be ready to use them to your advantage in the power interview.

Trend 1. Global Competition

What does the term *global competition* mean?_____

_____

_____

What experience do you personally have in dealing with people from other countries?_____

_____

_____

What involvement does the company you are interviewing with have with companies and markets of different countries?_____

_____

_____

What impact might increased global competition have on the work of the company you are approaching?_____

_____

_____

_____

Trend 2. The Flattening of Organizational Frameworks

How does the flattening of organizational frameworks change a person's access to career ladders in an organization?_____

_____

_____

_____

What does the organizational chart of the company you're approaching look like?_____

_____

_____

_____

Where does the position you are applying for fit on the company's current organizational chart?_____

_____

_____

_____

Trend 3. Managing Diversity

What is your ethnic background, and how does that affect the way you view the world?_____

_____

_____

_____

How does your being male or female affect the way you view the world and the workplace?_____

_____

_____

_____

What stereotyped attitudes do you hold about people different from yourself, and what can you do to rid yourself of them?_____

_____

_____

_____

What experiences have you had in working with people different from yourself, and how have you managed those relationships?_____

_____

_____

_____

Trend 4. Understanding and Using Computers

What types of computer hardware and software do you know how to

use?_____

_____

_____

How have you used computers in the past to make a work project

more efficient or effective?_____

_____

_____

Trend 5. Teams, Teams, Teams

Does the organization you're interviewing with have any formal team
development programs (for example, quality circles or employee in-

volvement)?_____

_____

_____

Have you been involved in work teams in the past or in any sort of
organized team activites (for example, sports or fundraising)? If so,

how successful were you?_____

_____

_____

_____

What skills do you have that would make you a valuable contributor to an organization's teamwork (for example, group dynamics or interpersonal communication)?_____

_____

_____

Trend 6. The Service Obsession

List ways in which you have provided extraordinarily good service to a customer or client in the past._____

_____

_____

_____

Does the company you're interviewing for have an articulated view on service (for example, in its organizational goals, mission statement, or slogan)? If so what does that tell you about that company's approach to service?_____

_____

_____

What do you have to say about your appreciation of the importance of service, and how can you articulate it in an interview?_____

_____

_____

_____

Trend 7. From Brawn to Brains

What experience have you had in the past in managing large amounts of information?_____

_____

_____

In what ways does the organization you're approaching depend on having up-to-date information? How does it go about getting it?_____

_____

_____

What information-gathering and organizing technologies are you familiar with (for example, networks or software programs) and how could you use them in your prospective organization?_____

_____

_____

Trend 8. Quality Is Job One

Does the company you're approaching have an articulated position on the importance of quality (for example, in its mission statement or slogan)? If so, what is its position?_____

_____

_____

_____

What experience do you have with quality assurance or quality control? Do you have any stories you can tell about contributing significantly to the quality of the development or delivery of a product or service? What are they?_____

_____

_____

_____

Trend 9. The Human Side

What do you know about what motivates people at work (other than money, which is a given), and what examples do you have that show you to be a good motivator of others?_____

_____

_____

_____

Do you have any experience creating work incentives in an organization? If you don't, what are your ideas about it? If you do, what are some examples?_____

_____

_____

What experiences do you have in your background that show that you have strong human relations skills?_____

_____

_____

Trend 10. Value-Added

What products and/or services does the company you're approaching consider to be its primary source of income?_____

_____

What organizational functions are considered critical to the delivery of the company's products and/or services?_____

_____

_____

What skills do you have to offer that make a direct contribution to this organization's production and delivery of services?_____

_____

_____

_____

Trend 11. Keep it Clean—Ethics in the Workplace

What is your personal code of ethics for the workplace?_____

_____

_____

Does the company you're approaching deal with any sensitive areas that might increase the need for a clearly articulated stance on ethics?

_____

_____

Does the company you're approaching include a statement on ethics in its mission statement or in any other formal literature? If so, what is its position?_____

_____

_____

Trend 12. Risky Business

What experiences do you have in your background that show you are capable of creative risk taking?_____

_____

_____

How does the company you're approaching view creativity and risk taking? Is there any evidence that those traits are valued in employees?_____

_____

_____

Remember, these are significant trends in almost every employer's mind. Bring them up whenever you get the chance and you will be seen as someone truly in tune with and capable of handling the challenges of the future.

5

Winning the Interviewer:
How to Read, Impress,
and Win Over
the Decision Makers

THE CLINCHER CONNECTION

While great effort is exerted to make the interview process as objective as possible, interviewers are only human. When asked how they decide between two equally qualified candidates for a position, the majority of corporate interviewers confess the truth. They pick the one with whom they feel the stronger connection. This somewhat fuzzy notion, "the connection," is worth your attention. As an interviewee you are faced with a difficult chore. Your job, in addition to answering questions in the strongest way possible, is to influence the person across from you into making a decision in your favor. Observers of human behavior and interpersonal relationships have spent many years trying to explain why each of us is more attracted to some people than to others. Explanations range from the scientific (genetics) to the ethereal (karma). Chances are good that relying on either of these extremes for a critical connection with your interviewer will leave you out in the cold. What is helpful, however, is to consider a variety of factors that could very well sway the interviewer in your favor.

Knowing Your Target

Knowing your target is an easy thing to do, yet most people don't take the time to do it when preparing for an interview. What it requires is a willingness and ability to search out information about your prospective target and to use that information in a way that sets you apart from the crowd.

For example, say you set as your target corporate giant AT&T. If you were not careful, you might think that you were approaching an organization that borders on being an old, established institution steeped in bureaucracy. You might, if you were not careful, have approached this organizataion as it existed prior to divestiture, as the regulated monopoly it once was, and make assumptions about its corporate culture based on that image. You'd be dead wrong—and dead in the water.

If you had done your homework, it's entirely possible that you would have read the cover story in the June 19, 1989, issue of *Fortune* magazine, featuring Bob Allen, the CEO of AT&T. In that article you would find that the operating procedure for AT&T is to adapt and adjust to change, not to stay the course. You'd find that there has been a dramatic shift in the way the organization is being run, away from the centralization of Allen's predecessor to a decentralized team approach. You'd learn that Donaldson, Lufkin, and Jenrette, a key consulting firm for AT&T stated, ''A lot of good young bulls below top management will carry the company into the 21st century.'' And with that information you'd have a much better chance of having a winning interview.

Understanding Organizational Cultures

Understanding the culture of the organization you are approaching can be a key to getting your foot in the door. Finding creative ways to reach the people with the power can set you apart from the crowd. For example, we heard of one man determined to get a job in a top advertising agency but unable to gain access to the decision makers in that organization. After several traditional approaches he decided to try something different. He took an old shoe of his, shined it up, and sent it to the prospective employer with a note that read, ''Just wanted to get my foot in the door.'' Now we wouldn't recommend this tactic to you for any other industry, but in this case it was the perfect entrance into an organization whose top concern is hiring people with imagination.

When you choose to work for a winning company you will

probably encounter an organization deeply entrenched in its culture. A company does not become one of the elite overnight. More than likely there are a range of organizational customs and rituals that define the company. Understanding what makes that organization tick before observing and responding to its customs in the course of the interview process can make all the difference in the world.

You can learn a great deal about an organization just by keeping your eyes open on your way to the interview. The physical surroundings, the building, the landscaping, the layout of the offices, and the content of the offices can tell you a great deal about the culture of the organization. Looking carefully at all these things will tell you a lot about what working in this organization might be like and can help you build your case for a match.

For example, we knew of one woman who was traveling around the country doing research on female presidents of small companies. She was on her way to see a woman who had started a very creative company and was surprised when she arrived at the entrance of a typical industrial park. She expected a much more aesthetically pleasing environment, given the nature of this woman's company. Her expectations were confirmed when, cruising through the mass of prefab aluminum warehouses, she spotted a white stucco building off in the woods adjacent to the park. She didn't have to check the address. She knew she had found her target.

The way the inside of the building, particularly the way work stations are set up, will tell you a lot about the culture of the organization as well. For example, walk into any traditional U.S. industrial factory and you'll see people lined up in rows of bolted-down tables performing their routine tasks. The supervisor will be walking up and down the aisles. The clock will be on the front wall, and bells will ring to signal breaks, lunch, and the ending of shifts. And they wonder why employees act like schoolchildren! The point is, the way work is doled out and set up will tell you a great deal about what working in that organization would be like and can help you navigate your interview.

Transfer the preceding scene to a corporate setting and you'll see what we mean. We know of one Fortune 500 insurance company where employees fight over inches of office space. Status is so tied to the amount and location of one's work space that no one will give an inch. One woman spent two months without a desk because the one to match her newly appointed position was not in stock; she refused to work at a smaller-sized one, and the company refused to give her an oversized one for the interim period. In this particular organization, with a little bit of keen observation, you could tell how valued the job you were applying for was by the location and dimensions of your work space.

Like the creative company started by the entrepreneur, the schoolhouse factory, and the territorial insurance office, the companies you approach will have settings that represent their culture and the values of their leaders. Pay close attention to these symbols and you will be on your way to determining the cultural pulse of the organization—and to making the connection you need to get the offers you want.

Comparing Apples and Oranges (or IBMs)

One of the common mistakes job seekers make is that once they've honed in on an industry they think they can approach all companies in that industry with the same strategy. A quick look at two companies in the same industry will illustrate the pitfalls of such a strategy. Say you've identified the computer industry as your primary target. You might very well apply to IBM and to Wang Laboratories. If you studied IBM you'd find a company steeped in tradition. The "old granddad" of computer companies, IBM and its leaders (and its marketers) see it as having a long tradition of excellence and dominance in the computer market. "Big Blue" as it is called by many, sees itself as most able to meet the needs of the computer-buying public by combining state-of-the-art technology with tried and true service delivery. Part of its corporate lore is the trouble-shooting team. If you have a problem with your IBM machine that is not taken care of through typical channels, let it be known to the powers that be. Shortly thereafter a team of trouble shooters in pin-striped suits will descend on your workplace to fix it. The response after they leave is akin to "who were those masked men?"

One of the ways IBM successfully perpetuates its corporate image is through the establishment and maintenance of clear norms, policies, and procedures for operating. This approach works for the company and is something that you as an interviewee and prospective employee must appreciate if you expect a serious chance of getting a job there.

However, to assume that all computer companies operate like IBM would be a great mistake, and approaching them in the same way would be an even greater mistake. Wang Laboratories, for example, has not been around as long as IBM, yet it has also managed to achieve prominence in the field. Relatively speaking, Wang is the new kid on the block. It prides itself on being able to deliver higher-quality products faster than other companies. Part of its marketing approach, and its organizational style, is to be able to tolerate ambiguity and adapt to change as the needs of the customer change. To do this it shies away from the sort of institutionalized norms, policies, and procedures so characteristic of IBM, favoring a much less formal mode of operation.

The more time you spent in each organization, the more apparent the differences would be. The more familiar you became with the companies, the more evident it would be to you that those doing the hiring in each look for decidedly different traits.

It's also important to realize that just as companies in the same industry are different from each other, so are units of the same company. The computer industry once again provides a good illustration. For example, I've worked with people from three different manufacturing plants of Digital Equipment Corporation. One of those plants is what might be called a traditional manufacturing setup with a traditional managerial hierarchy. The second plant is run with a participatory approach, in which people work in teams and there are very few managers. The third plant is in an urban center, and the large majority of employees are black or Hispanic, unlike the other two plants, which are mostly white. Each plant has its own culture and its own way of operating. The frame of reference can sometimes be dramatically different. On one occasion, a gathering of people from the various plants, I asked how things were going. The person from the traditonal plant said, ''Great, we're 20 percent above quota.'' The person from the participatory plant said, ''People are experiencing a lot of anger in the plant.'' The point is not that the participatory plant performs worse than the others—in fact, at times it outperforms the others. The important thing to realize is that the way people view and talk about what they do is different in the different plants.

Applicants applying for work in each of these settings would do well to know how that organization operates so that they might present themselves as a good match. You can be sure that the interviewer is looking for someone who will fit in.

Making Contact

Research on human behavior over the past 50 years suggests that different people view the world in different ways. While you may think this has nothing to do with the interview process, understanding and responding to these differences can help you. Consider the possibility that each of us is surrounded by a perceptual screen, a filter if you will, that processes what we see, hear, and feel a split second before we see, hear, or feel it. Being able to identify quickly the perceptual screen of the interviewer can go a long way in helping you make the critical connection.

One way to understand differences is through the use of neurolinguistic programming, or NLP. NLP is a simple method for reading a person's style that can greatly enhance your ability to connect with that person. Therapists have long used NLP as a way of making clients feel more at ease. It has recently enjoyed a great deal of success as a way for salespeople to make the all-important link with the customer. The link you make with an interviewer can help add to the impression that you might be a good person for that organization. Understanding and using NLP can help create that link.

One way to understand NLP is to examine the notion that by behaving in a certain way you can convince someone that you are a particular type of person. Great actors have long appreciated this simple truth. Consider the example of Dustin Hoffman in the movie *Rainman*. Anyone who has seen it can attest to Hoffman's mastery, his ability to persuade us that he was an autistic savant. It wasn't until I saw a rerun of "Sixty Minutes" that I realized what Hoffman had done. The TV segment profiled three savants, people with limited everyday skills who had achieved extraordinary mastery in a particular area, to the point of being called geniuses. One of the savants, like Hoffman's character in *Rainman*, had remarkable mathematical ability. The other remarkable thing about this was that he looked, sounded, and acted exactly like Hoffman's characterization of the savant. What Hoffman did, to persuade us we were watching a true savant, was to match his behavior, his sound, his actions, and his affect, to the point that we believed what we saw, heard, and felt while watching this movie.

Some psychologists would call this an example of behavior modeling. Behavior modeling is an approach to training developed by industrial psychologist Albert Bandura whereby a trainee masters a skill by closely observing and replicating the actions of a master. One of the side effects, and the payoff here, is that the trainee often appears to be actually like the person being modeled. If one of the ways to make a connection is to make the interviewer feel that you and he or she are alike, behavior modeling can help create that effect. While this may seem artificial to some of you, it is in fact merely a way to overcome the artificial barriers that are created by interviews. If it feels comfortable to you, use it; if not, don't—it wouldn't work anyway.

NLP can have a similar effect in creating a sense of connectedness with an interviewer. Although mastering NLP can take some time, the basic principles are simple. You can master NLP with some practice and find it helpful in all sorts of relationships beyond, as well as during, the interview. The key aspect of NLP involves identifying a person's primary sensory orientation. There are three basic orientations: visual, auditory, and kinesthetic. Visuals rely heavily on their eyes, and they like to "see" what it is they are thinking about. Auditories rely on their ears more, want to "hear" things clearly, and are more dependent on words for gaining understanding. Kinesthetics are more "hands on" and depend on "getting a feel" for something before passing judgment.

Here's an example of a simple way to identify a person's NLP orientation. I run a workshop series in a beautiful, old Victorian house. When new participants begin a series, I invariably get comments and questions about the setting. I can often tell from these comments and questions what a person's NLP style is. When someone says, "Look at this place; isn't it something?" I know I'm with a visual person. When someone asks, "What do you know about the history of this place?" I know I'm with an auditory person. When someone says, "Imagine what it was like living in this place years ago," I know I'm with a kinesthetic.

Imagine that you are in an interview for a job you really want. The questioning is going well, and you want to be sure to leave the interviewer with the feeling that you would be a good match for the position. One way to influence that interviewer is to identify what his or her primary orientation is (visual, auditory, or kinesthetic) and behave in a way that your interviewer best understands. This may sound like an unfair strategy, but it doesn't have to be. We're not suggesting that you "be someone you're not." That would probably backfire on you. What we're suggesting is that in this highly artificial situation and limited time (talk about unfair) you use all the resources available to you to make things go your way.

So if you're comfortable using this information this is how you might proceed. Pay attention to the language your interviewer uses when asking questions to determine whether you are sitting across from someone who is primarily visual, auditory, or kinesthetic.

Visuals are people who experience the world most dramatically through their eyes; consequently they also think and speak with visual cues. When presenting ideas, visuals are most likely to talk about how things "appear" to be. When zeroing in on an idea they would tend to talk about getting a "focus" on something. Visuals would present a scenario for you to respond to by giving you a "picture" of a situation. When asking you about your ideal job they might ask you what the perfect job situation would "look" like. When presenting difficult problems for you to solve they would ask you to "see" yourself in the situation. A visual interviewer might ask you about your "perspective" on a given organizational problem or ask you to "outline" your approach to solving that problem.

Auditories are people who experience the world most vividly through their ears; consequently they also think and speak with auditory cues. When presenting ideas they might ask you to "listen" carefully to understand a situation. When zeroing in on an idea they would tend to talk about really "tuning in" to what's going on. Auditories would present a scenario for you to respond to by asking you what a particular situation "sounds" like to you. When asking you about your ideal job they might ask to "hear" what you want out of a job. When presenting difficult problems for you to solve they would ask you to "discuss" possible solutions. An auditory interviewer might ask you to "elaborate" on your opinion on a given organizational problem or to "articulate" an approach to solving that problem.

Kinesthetics are people who are very tactile, who experience the world by "touching" and "feeling" what's going on around them; consequently they also think and speak with kinesthetic cues. When presenting ideas they might ask you to "get a feel" for a situation. When zeroing in on an idea they would tend to talk about really "getting in touch" with what's going on. Kinesthetics would present a scenario for you to respond to by asking you what you "sense" is happening. When asking you about your ideal job they might ask you where you think you might "fit" in the organization. When presenting difficult problems for you to solve they would ask what your "grasp" of the situation was. A kinesthetic interviewer might ask you to see if you could "get a handle" on a given organizational problem or "get hold of" an approach to solving that problem.

As you read these examples of different representational approaches, you probably found one of the three to be more "natural." Your response to each will be a clue to what your particular orientation is. The one that feels most comfortable is probably the one that matches your personal style. That's important to keep in mind because it's part of who you are and how you communicate. More important though is being able to read others' orientations so that you can respond to them in a way that leaves the impression that you at least understood them and at best identified with them.

As you can see from these examples, people with a visual, auditory, or kinesthetic orientation will present a broad range of ideas and scenarios without deviating from their primary orientation. One way to begin to use NLP effectively for interviewing is to create a list of words you might use if you were operating in a particular mode. The preceding examples each used seven different words or phrases typical of the particular orientation. Think of some others and keep them in mind the next time you're talking with someone. You'll be amazed at how easily you can identify whether someone is visual, auditory, or kinesthetic.

Another way to understand differences and to make a connection by overcoming them is to pay attention to the extent to which people are action-oriented versus observant and feeling-oriented versus cognitive. Many years ago psychologist Carl Jung postulated that these two continua—active versus observant and feeling versus thinking—were the basis for understanding key differences in human nature. Since then many theorists have developed models about learning and human behavior based on the Jungian concept. While it would be pointless to elaborate on those models here, there is an aspect of Jung's model that can be useful for the job seeker in the selection interview.

Imagine once again that you are sitting across from an interviewer and the questioning is going well. You are interested in finding a way to make that all-important link with the person opposite you. There are two things you can pay attention to that will help you make a stronger connection: Is the person feeling- or thinking-oriented, and is the person action-oriented or observant?

People who are feeling-oriented will demonstrate an interest in the "people side" of a given situation. They will focus on the elements of a problem that involve the impact on the human factor. Their concern, regardless of the problem, will tend to be on how its outcome will affect the players involved. They are not necessarily more humanitarian than others; they just bring a perspective to situations that highlights the impact on people and their responses.

People who are thinking-oriented tend to focus more on the task at hand than on the people involved. They tend to think analytically about potential outcomes of a situation in terms of the product or project in question. Their concern, regardless of the problem, is on what the concrete results will be. They are not necessarily less concerned about people; they just tend to look at situations from a bottom-line perspective.

In addition to the feeling-thinking continuum that differentiates some interviewers from others, there is also the active-observant continuum.

People who are action-oriented like to focus on immediate results. They tend to forgo the long range for the short term. They are more likely to be concerned with the impact of a decision on the present than on its far-reaching ramifications. They are more concerned with the here and now than with the future. While they can appreciate the importance of long-range planning, it is not their top priority.

People who are observant tend to think analytically and systematically. They are concerned with the whole picture and with the long term. They know that results matter, but they believe that the means by which those results are attained will, in the long run, also make a difference. Like the chess player, people who are observant tend to think in terms of steps and are focused on the impact of each step on subsequent moves.

Now you may be thinking that any successful business-person will, out of necessity, be all of the preceding, depending on the situation. You would be right. However, it also seems to be true that most people have a tendency to be more on one end of each continuum than on the other most of the time. Paying attention to whom you're talking to, and paying attention to the end of the continuum they seem to be working from, is important. It can help you to understand them, effectively respond to them, and ultimately, win them over.

The Importance of World View

Interviews by design are person-to-person encounters. No matter how objective the process is made to seem, ultimately people are judging people. Since this is so, it is reasonable to assume that the judgments the interviewer makes about the interviewee are key to the outcome. Ideally, the key judgments relate to the key aspects of the job. Unfortunately, the key judgments sometimes relate more to personal characteristics than to professional ones.

You are who you are, and there's no point in projecting an image that differs dramatically from that authentic self. However, if the subjective side of interviewing is, as we suspect, essentially Russian roulette, then it makes sense, for your own survival, to pay attention to who the other players are. One way to understand your interviewer, and perhaps to make the critical link we've talked about in this chapter, is to pay attention to and respond to that person's world view. A world view is essentially a set of beliefs and attitudes a person has about a range of universal concerns. Discovering an interviewer's world view can be particularly helpful if you find yourself sitting across from someone with whom you have little in common.

The concept of world view is simply a way of organizing information about one's perspective on a range of issues, a way to sort out who it is who is sitting across from you. One's world view includes knowledge, beliefs, and attitudes about politics, religion, sports, family, education, money, and a host of other topics. Paying attention to your interviewer's positions on each of these areas can help you make the personal link that makes the critical difference.

It is amazing how calling on some aspect of world view can sometimes turn a difficult situation into a harmonious one. For example, I was recently at a luncheon meeting with a colleague. The two of us were working on a major contract with a client who to date had been rather reticent about our relationship. On the way to the meeting my colleague and I were discussing our client's coolness and planning a strategy that might turn things around. Since there seemed to be no problems pertaining to the work we were doing, we decided to get through the business of the meeting as soon as possible and keep our ears open for any opportunities to connect through our world views. During dessert I asked the client if he had any children. His face lit up as he began talking about his daughter and her swim team. My colleague, an avid, award-winning swimmer in high school, chimed in with all her knowledge about swimming, coaching, and the current state competitions. We spent the next half hour talking about our families, and we left the meeting feeling more comfortable than we had ever felt before with this client. Our subsequent project with this client proved to be highly successful. The work was done in an extremely enthusiastic, cooperative mode. We attribute some of that success to the connection we made that day through our world views.

While you may not always get an opportunity to compare world views with an interviewer, paying attention to who that person is and looking for opportunities to connect can make all the difference. Following are some of the key world view categories to keep in mind.

Politics   Politics is probably one of the stickier world-view categories. More than divulging whether you are a Democrat or Republican is at stake here. If you're not careful you may present a bias that is perceived as contrary to the needs of the organization. A good rule of thumb is to avoid making any statements that commit you to any political position. However, listening for cues to the interviewer's potential leanings can shed light on who this person is and what his or her priorities are. One man we know who was head of his previous organization's union drive highlighted his union work in his résumés and interviews. He had a very difficult time finding work. Just when he was about to change his approach he was interviewed by someone who had been a union organizer in his early years. That was the last interview he needed.

The Arts   During a recent vacation I asked an 18-year-old on my block to watch my house while I was gone. I was new to the neighborhood and had just met the young man. He seemed very competent and responsible, yet a bit uncomfortable with me. I knew his family and figured he was concerned about doing a good job. When I returned I asked him to come by so I could pay him and tell him what a great job he had done. When he came in he still seemed a bit nervous. I noticed he was wearing a Bob Dylan T-shirt from a recent concert tour. Early in our conversation I mentioned that when I was growing up I was a big Dylan fan and had a large collection of his albums. He got very excited, we talked about music for a while, and he left feeling a much greater connection to me than he had when he walked in.

Many people have enthusiasms, some passions, for certain artists or arts activities. Often they love meeting other people who share that enthusiasm and feel an immediate kinship. Opera buffs love to meet other opera buffs; Grateful Dead enthusiasts (Deadheads) love to meet other Deadheads; stamp collectors love to meet other stamp collectors. More than similarity is involved here. People often feel that they learn something about someone when they uncover their enthusiasms. While these interests are not always visible or available to you, they sometimes do become evident if you're paying attention to comments, objects in the office, and so on.

Sports   Like it or not, chances are if you're sitting across from someone who has been successful in the corporate world, that person knows a reasonable amount about sports. While you may believe (rightfully so) that this has nothing to do with your potential performance, ignorance in this area can hurt you. The problem is that quite often talk of sports, like the weather, is used to break the ice or to fill gaps in time. Unless you have a basic understanding of the major U.S. sports—baseball, football, basketball, and yes, golf—you may find yourself embarrassingly without comment when the interviewer tries to make you feel more at ease. Although lack of knowledge in this area is not the kiss of death, it is worth your while to gain an understanding of the basics. (We heard of one interviewee who mistook talk of a Giant touchdown as conversation about the space shuttle.)

In America sports serve as a metaphor for business. Creative people in business will often use sports analogies to gain insight into a particular organizational problem or scenario. If you don't understand the basics of sports you may find yourself too often wondering what everyone is talking about.

The Family   In the past the sanctity and value of the family was unquestioned. While this can still be a world-view category that makes a connection (as illustrated in the story earlier in this chapter), that is not always the case. In the past it would be fairly safe for an applicant to expound effusively on the importance of family in his or her career. Many things have changed that view, however, including the proliferation of dual-career families and the concern that the individual may be stretched by too many family demands. While families are gaining ground in their efforts toward corporate-supported child care, other trends are emerging simultaneously that give families less clout.

Many companies are concerned about the extent to which a person is family-focused versus career-focused. Recent developments such as the "Mommy track," the notion that women with families should be on different career tracks than those without, demonstrate this concern. While it's okay to care about your family, most employers still want to believe that the company and the job come first. Also it is entirely possible that the person sitting across from you doesn't have a family to care for and may not share or understand your commitment.

Paying attention to the interviewer's cues about attitudes toward family can tell you whether or not this world-view category is one for a potential connection or not.

Money   If you're applying for work in the free-enterprise system you are most likely going to encounter people whose concern for making money is fairly high on their list of priorities. Beyond this basic concern for turning a profit, however, you will find a range of attitudes about money and the discussion of financial matters. It is safe to say that the closer the business is to finance-related endeavors, the more that talk of money will be evident. In industries such as banking, investments, and insurance you are likely to hear people talk at length about money because essentially it is their product. The further you get from the "money industries" the more difficult it is to discern the distinction between greed and ambition. While some people are open books about their personal finances and would not hesitate to talk about their personal activities, say, in the stock market, others would consider it a violation of their privacy. Paying attention to expressed attitudes about money in the course of a conversation will tell you which aspects of it the interviewer is comfortable with and which are off limits. Although you may not find the occasion to talk about money in an interview, there may be times when a common perspective will surface, creating the opportunity to form another link with the interviewer.

OVERCOMING DIFFERENCES IN AN INTERVIEW

In addition to your world view, there are other factors having to do with who you actually are that can work for or against you. Although you have no control over these actual characteristics, you do have some control over how they are perceived.

While the old adage "great minds think alike" may or may not be true, what seems to be true quite often is that "like minds think alike." There's a good chance that the more similar you and your interviewer are in age, race, socioeconomic background, educational background, and gender, the more easily you'll be able to make a critical connection. However, being different from your interviewer in any (or all) of these categories is no reason for despair. It is a reason for attention. By paying attention to the differences between yourself and the interviewer, your chances of getting through to that person—in spite of your differences—increase dramatically.

Age

I had a woman in my office today, concerned about getting work. "Who would want to hire a 47-year-old woman," she lamented. I recently heard the same fear expressed from a graying 48-year-old man. The problem, I told them both, is not their age but the attitude about their age that they bring to an interview. I've seen countless men and women lose job opportunities, not because of their age, but because of the way they present their age. Statements such as "I would bring a tremendous amount of experience to this position" work much better than "I know I'm older than the typical candidate but. . . ."

If you're sitting across from an interviewer considerably older than you, you probably need to convince him or her that you have the maturity to do the job. If you're sitting across from someone considerably younger than you, you need to convey that you are not after his or her job and that you have no problem reporting to someone younger. If you and the interviewer are a similar age, you may find a sense of camaraderie that you can tap for making a connection. However, you want to be careful; some interviewers will resent any assumptions based on age. Also you want to be sure to let the interviewer know that you can handle reporting to a peer.

Socioeconomic Background and Status

While there is no explicit class system in this country, people find ways to identify with and differentiate themselves from certain groups. For example, certain people take pride in coming from a working-class background, whereas others pride themselves on their privileged lineage. In addition, people find ways to express their socioeconomic status by the types of clothing and jewelry they wear, the cars they drive, and even the way they wear their hair. People often make assumptions about others, whether true or false, by paying attention to the artifacts of socioeconomic background. Focusing on the socioeconomic artifacts of the person interviewing you will often give you information on who that person is or at least who he or she would like to be.

If you find yourself sitting across from someone whose background seems similar to yours, you may find ways in the course of an interview to let that be known. If you sense that the two of you are vastly different, avoid highlighting the differences. Remember, in general people are more comfortable with people they perceive are like them than those they perceive to be different.

Race

Racial similarities and differences are probably the most difficult personal characteristics to deal with. In a culture dominated by whites there is pressure, regardless of your race, to behave in a way typical to the dominant group. If both the interviewer and the interviewee are white, you probably won't even think about race during the interview. Awareness of racial differences becomes evident when either the interviewer or the interviewee or both are of a racial background other than white. The important thing to remember here is that if the person interviewing you is from a racial background different from yours, he or she may have ways of communicating that are unfamiliar to you.

People often find, when they take a close look at racial differences, that different groups have different norms concerning eye contact, personal distance, body language, and other subtle aspects of communication.

The important thing when trying to overcome racial differences with interviewers is to follow their lead in the course of communication. This does not mean mimicking them, which will certainly backfire on you. What it does mean is allowing them to establish some norms concerning the way the two of you communicate. Doing this will demonstrate your ability to communicate with someone different from yourself, will make them more comfortable, and will avoid potentially embarrassing and damaging mistakes.

Educational Background

As with socioeconomic background, some people carry with them an academic identity reflecting a certain level of status. Depending on how prestigious a school you attended, you may find that you have access to certain organizations more easily than do others. Those of you who have attended a prestigious school will find that your access does not diminish over time. I recently worked with a client who graduated from Harvard in 1959. He was looking for work in a new field and was having trouble finding it. He was startled when I encouraged him to tap his university alumni association for contacts—after all, it had been 30 years. He did call his association, and to his surprise it was very responsive and very helpful.

Those of you who don't have a prestigious school in your background need to be aware of bias when approaching an organization that has a history of hiring people from certain schools. Do not make the mistake of thinking that you are out of the running—exceptions are made every day. As with the age issue, the extent to which you rise above this potential short-coming will determine your success. If you find yourself competing with Ivy Leaguers and you yourself are not one, be sure to emphasize the quality of the education you received and how you managed to get it.

Gender

Men have long been the dominant sex (at least overtly) in the workplace. Over the past 30 years women have made considerable headway. It is now entirely possible (although statistically unlikely) that you could be interviewed for a high-level position by a woman.

If you are a man and find yourself across from a woman interviewer, you need to be aware that one of her concerns is that you are comfortable reporting to a woman. The corporate workplace is still dominated by men, and many women have been burned by men who use gender as a weapon against them.

If you are a woman being interviewed by a man, your task is to convince him that you are as aggressive and driven as the male competition.

If you are a woman and your interviewer is a woman, chances are she has had to face many hurdles to get where she is. Don't assume that being a woman will help you. Most reports suggest that women who have succeeded are at least as hard as men on other women on the way up. Chances are you will have to prove to her that you can contribute to the company.

If both the interviewer and the interviewee are male, you probably won't even think about gender in the course of the interview—unless of course you are applying for a job as a secretary.

GIVING YOURSELF AWAY

It is essential to remember that what you are doing in an interview is selling yourself. One of the key elements of effective sales is knowing and responding to the customer and his or her needs, interests, and values. You may not know it but car dealers do this all the time. In most places, when you walk into an automobile showroom you will be sized up by your age, sex, the way you dress, the car you drove in with, and the way you operate from the time you get out of your car until the time you enter the showroom. Based on this analysis you will be confronted with a salesperson whom the dealership's demographers (they may not call themselves this) decide will be most likely to "pitch" you successfully. Imagine that you are the dealer and the car buyer is your interviewer. Although this may seem to be a reversal, in actuality it mirrors the interview situation in many ways. Although the car buyer must persuade the salesperson that the buying potential is there, the onus is on the salesperson, like the applicant, to convince the other that the product is worth the price.

YOU ARE WHAT YOU SAY

Another angle on this subject has to do with the notion that you, the applicant, are trying to present yourself as someone who fits the desires of the organization. Once again we can look at sales strategies to gain insight into how this is done. Imagine for a moment that the interviewer is a consumer of stereo equipment and you, the applicant, are a stereo merchant. It doesn't take a very trained eye to see that different stereo stores, through the image they project, appeal to different consumers.

A quick glance through the yellow pages reveals three names, Crazy Eddie, Sound Playground, and Scientific Stereo. A brief analysis of each name brings up some fairly safe assumptions. If I am most interested in price I go to Crazy Eddie (whose motto was ''my prices are insane''). If I am interested in equipment with lots of ''bells and whistles'' I go to Sound Playground. If I am interested in high-quality sound without the frills I go to Scientific Stereo. What's happening here is that each name, each consisting of two words, says a great deal about the image of that store and creates significant assumptions about the potential match between the seller's and the buyer's needs. The point is you need to have a clear understanding of who your interviewer is and what his or her needs and desires are in order to persuade that person that you are right for the company.

POWER PREP STRATEGY V

Organizational Cultures

This chapter discussed the importance of understanding the organization you're approaching by understanding its organizational culture. Cultural information can be found by reading the organization's literature, visiting the organization prior to an interview, conducting preliminary interviews, and talking with people who work there. Uncover the following information about the organization you are approaching and you will have a good grasp of its culture and of what working there would be like.

Who is the CEO of the organization you are approaching and what is that person like? (You can gather this information from news clips, informal conversation, networking, and so on.) _____

_____

_____

What does the way the building looks like tell you about the organization's culture? _____

_____

_____

What does the way the employees dress tell you? _____

_____

_____

What does the setup of the offices tell you? _____

_____

_____

What do the internal modes of communication (for example, employee newsletters and bulletin boards) tell you? _____

_____

_____

What does the organization's image tell you? _____

_____

_____

What does the allocation of resources (who gets what) tell you about the organization? _____

_____

_____

What does the reward system tell you about who is valued? _____

_____

_____

Understanding the Interviewer's Style

In the discussion on neurolinguistic programming you were told that some people are visual, some auditory, and some kinesthetic. What ways do you personally have for identifying each of the NLP styles.

Visual _____

_____

Auditory _____

_____

Kinesthetic _____

_____

What is your personal NLP style? _____

_____

In Carl Jung's model on different types of people you were told that some people are more feeling-oriented and some more thinking-oriented. You were also told that some people are more action-oriented and some more observant. What ways do you personally have for telling what a person's particular orientation is?

Feeling-oriented _____

_____

Thinking-oriented _____

_____

Action-oriented _____

_____

Observant _____

_____

Which of the four types in Jung's model most reflects your personal style?

Feeling/action-oriented   Thinking/action-oriented

Feeling/observant   Thinking/observant

What are the implications of your style on your performance in an

interview? _____

_____

World View

What is your personal world view on politics, and to what extent is it likely to match or clash with the politics of your interviewer? _____

_____

_____

Who are your favorite arts figures, what are your favorite arts activities, and to what extent are these likely to be accepted and respected in the place you're interviewing? _____

_____

_____

What do you know about the major U.S. sports, what is your attitude about sports, and what if any metaphors do you use comparing the nature of sports to the nature of business? _____

_____

_____

_____

To what extent are you able to balance work and family, and how can you show that your family's needs do not interfere with your work requirements? _____

_____

_____

_____

To what extent are you comfortable discussing money matters? How might your knowledge of and comfort in discussing personal finances hinder or help your "connecting" in an interview? _____

_____

_____

_____

Overcoming Differences

To what extent do you consider your age to be an asset or liability in
an interview? In what ways can you use your age to "connect" in an

interview? _____

_____

_____

What significance does your socioeconomic background have on your
position as an applicant? How might you use it to your advantage?

_____

_____

_____

What significance does your racial background have on who you are?

_____

_____

What do you know about racial differences that can help you "con-

nect" in an interview with someone of a different race? _____

_____

_____

In what ways does your educational background strengthen or weaken your position as an applicant? How can you compensate for the weakness or capitalize on the strength? _____

_____

_____

_____

How does your being a man or a woman affect your sense of who you are? How does that affect your performance in an interview? _____

_____

_____

How might your gender influence your chances in an interview? What can you do to neutralize any assessment based on gender? _____

_____

_____

Choosing a Work Style: Finding the Right Places to Interview

In writing this book we make the assumption that those who are interested in power interviewing are also interested in using their personal power to get the best jobs. What constitutes the best jobs depends on your own needs and desires. In a country such as ours that is rich in opportunity, there are many places to find the sort of success you can gain by harnessing your personal resources. In this book we have chosen to focus on work in the free-enterprise system—the business world. However, within that realm there are many types of organizations and jobs that vary in their scope and expectations. In looking at the different types of jobs in different settings we make two assumptions: one, that you want to make a decent living, and two, that you want a reasonable degree of job satisfaction. Beyond that there are a range of variables to consider when making decisions about where to interview. This chapter discusses the types of environments you might pursue, and what you might find in each. Also included are suggestions for questions to ask in an interview and guidelines for negotiating the best deal possible once you've decided what you want.

IN SEARCH OF THE SILVER PORSCHE

One of the most important decisions you'll make in the interview process is whether or not a particular job and organization matches your requirements.

Fred worked for one of the large Fortune 500 computer

companies. Being considered for a promotion, he was scheduled to be interviewed by a team of vice presidents. Fred liked
his work but always had a nagging feeling about wanting to be
his own boss. He decided to take two weeks off before his
interview and travel across the country. One day while traveling
on Route 80 he passed a couple in a Winnebago with a Porsche
in tow. "This man has attained what I strive for," he thought. A
few miles down the road he saw the man pull off into a rest
area. "A chance to meet my role model," he thought, and
pulled off behind him.

Fred approached the man and told him of his situation, the
impending promotion, and his reservations. "Don't take it,"
said the man. "There isn't a day that goes by when I don't look
at that Porsche and resent what it cost me." Fred went home,
quit his job, and opened a small computer store, where he is his
own boss.

If you have been reading this book you're probably not
compelled, at least at this point in your life, to quit working for
a company and start your own business. We didn't tell you this
story to encourage you to do so. What's important about Fred's
story is that he based his decision about whether or not he
would take the job on what he wanted most from work.

If you're doing a good job at getting interviews and performing well in them, you will get offers that you should turn
down. You should turn them down not because they are bad
offers but rather because at this point in your career they are not
a good match for you. That is not easy to do, especially if you
are unemployed. However, in the long run, waiting for a job
that is a good match will serve you better, and probably lead to
the need for fewer interviews in the future. Use as your basis for
your decision in an interview the extent to which the work
itself, and working in that organization, excites you. In making
that decision you'll avoid a great deal of retrenching and ma-
neuvering because of a bad decision.

QUALITY OF WORK LIFE

One advantage of the diverse U.S. marketplace is that there are
choices. Shifting demographics and predicted shortages in

many fields mean that for the talented applicant it is a buyer's market. In addition to the kind of company you want, there's a good chance you can choose, to some extent, the kind of work you do. Although most good jobs require a range of focus points, they usually do emphasize one aspect of work life more than others. It makes sense to consider jobs that best match your true desires. Your genuine enthusiasm will help you in the interview and lead to more exciting offers.

Mastery

As mentioned earlier most organizations are seeking people who can perform a broad range of tasks. However, some jobs, by definition, require a mastery of a particular knowledge base or area of expertise. If what you want most in a job is to be responsible for knowing everything there is to know about a particular subject, go for the jobs that seem highly specialized. The best way to identify these jobs is by title and specifications. The more specific and detailed the job description, the more likely the company is looking for someone who likes to be immersed in a specific discipline. During an interview pay attention to the depth and detail of the questioning in a particular subject matter. This, too, will indicate that the company is looking for someone able to be a master of a given technology.

Exploration

Whereas some jobs demand mastery of known technology, other jobs are more open-ended. If what you want is opportunity to explore the unknown and discover new ways of operating, go for the exploratory jobs. The best way to identify these is to look for jobs whose descriptions are fairly vague. Employers who are looking for people to uncover new ways of operating often don't have a clear way of describing what it is they are looking for and who it is they want to do it. If in the course of the interview you find the interviewer's descriptions of the duties vague and unclear, you may very well have found an exploratory job. If the interviewer asks a lot of questions about your ability to tolerate ambiguity and your willingness to work in unstructured situations, you're on the right track.

Protection

If you're someone who cares about quality control, the "protection jobs" may be for you. Protection jobs can take many forms, including auditing, monitoring, observing, and even managing. People in protection jobs find themselves occupied with maintaining the quality of products and services by functioning in an overseer capacity. The best way to identify these jobs is to look for signs of the organization's concern with your ability to be trusted, your attention to detail, and your sense of rightness or fairness. In hiring for protection jobs interviewers will be particularly careful to ask questions that reveal information about your character.

Caretaking

As companies become increasingly concerned with the human side, one area of growing consideration is motivation. Having employees who know how people tick and can stimulate productivity will be critical. If what you like to do most is to help others develop their full potential, these are the kinds of jobs to go after. Whether you find yourself in a management role or a support role, there are many places in the contemporary organization for the caretaker. The best way to spot these jobs is to look for job descriptions that talk about motivation, productivity, teamwork, and high performance. Chances are employers looking to fill jobs with people who can address these concerns are trying to fill caretaker jobs. Pay particular attention in interviews for questions about your ability to manage relationships, handle conflict, and deal with difficult people.

Work Styles of the Rich and Famous

Regardless of the type or size of organization you choose to pursue, if you're going for the power positions there are things you should realize. Certain attitudes pervade among those who make it to the top of their field. When Donald Trump, arguably the most entrepreneurial and, to some, most envied man in America, went to the Milton Bradley Company to unveil his new board game, "Trump, The Game," his speech to the workers was revealing. Put in overtime, work hard, and you can make it was his message. It's that spirit of commitment of time and effort that you will find those in power expecting of those below them. Listen to his wife, Ivana, talk about her supervision of the transformation of the Plaza Hotel and you will realize that neither of these two is lacking in energy toward identified projects. Obviously this couple has tremendous resources at their fingertips. That's not the point. The point is, even though they could easily sit back and do nothing, they choose highly ambitious projects to work on, projects that they have the resources to complete but nonetheless are ambitious enough so that there is a possibility of failure.

Work, Work, Work

In case you think that the Trumps are unusual in their embrace of the traditional work ethic, consider the words of the leaders of several Fortune 500 companies as reported in the July 3, 1989, issue of *Fortune* magazine:

> I don't think the important traits for good managers have changed very much . . . hard work. . . .
>
> *Robert O. Anderson*
> *CEO Atlantic Richfield*

> Too many people today only want to put in a 40 hour week. . . . I always told my managers that you can't be successful unless you tell your [spouse] not to expect you home for dinner.
>
> *C. Kemmons Wilson*
> *Founder of Holiday Inn*

The same old qualities are necessary. . . . You have to be dedicated. . . .

> John E. Swearingen Jr.
> CEO Standard Oil.

If I find people who can tell me what's on TV at 8:15 on Thursday night, then I'm not interested in hiring them.

> René C. McPherson
> Former chief executive, Dana Corporation

I feel every person can have everything if they are willing to work, work, work.

> Estée Lauder

Whether you agree with these visions of what it takes to be successful in America or not is irrelevant. If you are interested in securing work in the better companies you must listen to these leaders. The people quoted and others like them set the tone for the organizations they run. If you want to convince those doing the hiring that you are right for their organization you must approach your intended organization with a sense of zeal akin to the preceding statements.

The Fortune 500

One of your richest options is to pursue work in the Fortune 500. There are many advantages to working for such a company, as well as some disadvantages. You should think about both before deciding to go ahead. You should also be prepared to respond to your interviewer's inquiries regarding these factors.

Some of the advantages of working in the Fortune 500 are these:

- The pay and benefits are generally better than similar jobs in small companies.
- They tend to have many locations and can give you a choice of where you want to live.
- They often have training programs that can further develop your future marketability.

- They can provide an impressive notch on your résumé and open doors to other companies.
- They can often offer other opportunities if you decide to shift into another area.

Some of the disadvantages of working in the Fortune 500 are these:

- Mergers, buyouts, and acquisitions could cause you to lose your position.
- The demands on your time may be more than you want to give. Fortune 500 companies typically expect employees to put in long hours.
- Because of their status, internal competition for the good jobs is often fierce.
- You may be asked to relocate against your will.

Perhaps the most important question you should ask yourself when considering work in the Fortune 500 is how central to your life do you want your job to be. While people who have chosen to work in these highly successful companies revel in their benefits, it's important to realize the full scope of their commitment. For example, most companies are realizing the need for providing adequate support for child care as increasing numbers of women are entering and staying in the work force. While you can expect some sort of support, whether in the form of an on-site day-care center or a child care subsidy, don't make the mistake of thinking that your family's welfare is the company's top priority. No company has made it to the exclusive ranks of the Fortune 500 by placing humanitarian concerns first. This is not a criticism; it is simply a reality. Although many companies have very generous benefit packages, their purpose is to lure the most talented, most aggressive workers. Be assured that if you are one of the fortunate applicants to be employed by a Fortune 500 company, you will earn your salary. One of the ways you will earn it is by putting your organization's needs first, even at times at the expense of your own family. Being very clear about your reasons for wanting to work in the Fortune 500 can make a great deal of difference during the interview, when you're trying to persuade someone that you're a good match. It will also help you ultimately decide whether or not to take the job.

Achievement Motivation

If you are highly motivated, unless you're thinking of starting your own business, the Fortune 500 may be your best primary source of jobs. One of the ways to measure whether or not the Fortune 500 is right for you is to consider the extent to which you are motivated to achieve. Psychologist David McLelland and his colleagues at Harvard University have spent years studying achievement motivation. Their research shows that some people are clearly more highly motivated to achieve than others. The researchers have devised a variety of simple tests to determine achievement motivation. For example, one test involves a ring toss game. Participants are asked to play the game with the goal of winning. They are then left to decide, on their own, how they will play. Some people, concerned with not losing, stand as close to the post as possible and get a large number of points. Others, determined to push the limits of possibility, stand as far away as possible, hoping to turn a long shot into a success. The third group takes a middle ground, standing far enough away to be challenged yet close enough to be likely to get a good number of the rings on the post. It is this third group that McLelland would call achievement-motivated. These people, willing to take calculated risks but careful to ensure success, are the type of people likely to thrive in a Fortune 500 environment. It is this type of success-oriented person that the Fortune 500 companies seek to employ because it is the orientation that matches the companies' commitment to high performance.

Up and Coming Companies

If you can't get a job in the Fortune 500 or one of the similarly established companies—or don't want one—other options are available. You may choose to pursue companies that are just getting started or are on their way up. There can be many advantages to such organizations. A company that is hungry for success is more likely to tap the resources of hungry employees, and to a greater extent, than companies that are steeped in tradition. Procuring a position in an organization in the process of creating its traditions can provide an exciting and rich period for your career. You may end up staying in the organization as it matures, or you may take what you've learned elsewhere. In any event, being involved in the growth of an organization will teach you a great deal about the ways of the business world. You'll be a much more knowledgeable businessperson once you've helped a company to grow, and consequently more marketable.

Support Industries

Most people think of the corporate world as primarily offering products and services to the public, but there is another, growing subsector. This growth area offers many fruitful opportunities to potential employees. Many companies, forced to tighten their belts, have chosen to have certain functions performed by outside firms. This has led to an unprecedented growth of support industries, companies whose function is to provide services no longer performed in-house. If your areas of expertise and interest include accounting, human resources, public relations, or a range of other support roles, chances are good of finding work in a firm offering these services. The nice thing about working in one of these organizations is that since their product is accounting, human resources, public relations, and so forth, employees who perform these functions are considered highly valued employees who contribute directly to the bottom line. This is quite a different position from providing one of these services in-house and being seen as on the periphery of what's really important.

Small Businesses

The small business is by many accounts the wave of the future. According to MIT professor David Birch, smaller firms, companies with fewer than 20 employees, create 98 percent of all new jobs in America. This staggering statistic has many implications for those seeking work. While the figures may be misleading—"new jobs" does not mean new openings to fill old jobs—the fact remains that small organizations offer opportunities to those interested in working in them. When you work for a small company you have a much better chance of gaining a sense of ownership in the company. Chances are you'll have more of a say in how the organization is run and how it does its business. In fact the small business model is increasingly being recognized as superior to the unwieldy corporate giant, to the extent that even large companies are trying to replicate it by decentralizing their bureaucracies. However, no matter how decentralized a corporation gets it still cannot replicate the dynamism, independence, and entrepreneurial spirit so much a part of the small business. If those are the things that excite you, remember the words of E. F. Schumacher: "Small is beautiful."

Creating a Winning Match

When making decisions about which companies to interview with, it is important—for the sake of the interview and the subsequent work—that you choose organizations that are a good match. In this book we've chosen to focus on interviewing in the free-enterprise system—with companies for whom the bottom line is the bottom line. While most of the material in this book can help improve your interviewing performance in the public sector as well, we assume that you are looking for work that provides high earning potential. Many people make the mistake of letting financial concerns exclusively guide their decisions. As illustrated in the story of the Porsche at the beginning of this chapter, this sort of blind fortune hunting can backfire.

One way to sort your good targets from less attractive ones is to consider what types of products and services appeal to you and which don't. This is not always as easy as it sounds. For example, you might be drawn to General Electric, whose motto, "We Bring Good Things to Life," might lead you to believe that you would be working for an organization whose primary thrust is providing products to improve the general quality of life. You might be surprised to learn, once you started working there, that the large majority of products it produces are for military use. While this may or may not cause problems for you personally, it could make a great deal of difference in whether or not you approach that company and how aggressively you pitch "who you are" in the interview.

In addition to understanding the major emphasis of an organization you would be wise to identify and understand its current thrust. For example, Tom's Toothpaste is a relatively small company that over the years has created a devoted following by pitching its "all natural" toothpaste to a select group of people interested in natural products. Knowing this little bit of information, you might present yourself in an interview as someone committed to meeting the consumer needs of this select group.

The problem with this approach is that Tom's has recently undergone a shift in strategy, is expanding its market, and is trying to appeal to "the average consumer." Its product has begun showing up on the shelves in CVS, Stop and Shop, and other major chains. Its marketers are hoping to capture a substantial share of the natural toothpaste market by appealing to the average person, increasingly concerned about health.

Say you were applying for a position in the expanding marketing department of Tom's because you enjoyed marketing to nontraditional markets. If in the interview you expressed interest by showing your knowledge of the alternative market, you would fall flat on your face. If you really wanted to work with nontraditional markets you would be very frustrated working at Tom's at this time. Since they have shifted their marketing thrust they are no longer a good match for you.

Beware of the Family Business

Estimates vary, but it is quite clear that many U.S. companies, both large and small, are family-run businesses. Working for a family business when you are not a member of the family is fine, provided the key people responsible for running the company are open to outsiders. Nothing is more frustrating to a rising employee than finding the way up cut short by family politics. Histories of companies both large and small are full of cases where family members were given jobs they couldn't handle. Consider the case of Wang Laboratories. Wang is such a large enterprise that most observers would not even consider it a family business, but they would be wrong. In 1986 An Wang, founder of the company, named his son Fred president, in spite of the fact that many observers both inside and outside the company felt it was a bad move. In 1989, three short years after he became president, Fred Wang was forced to resign, unable, many observers suggested, to follow in his father's footsteps. One can only speculate whether there were other candidates more capable of leading Wang.

The point is that many qualified candidates have lost positions because a family member who was less qualified was given preferential treatment. Nothing is more frustrating than finding your hard-earned promotion short-circuited by the family bloodline. A family business can be a great place to work. Although you may not find yourself vying for president with members of your company's family in the near future, you want to make sure that if the company you are joining is family-owned and -run, there is opportunity for outsiders.

Demands on Time

There was a time, not too long ago, when people in all different walks of life talked about the possibility of working fewer hours, perhaps even creating a four-day work week as the new standard. Like many well-meaning predictions this is one that, at least for the present, is far from becoming a reality. If you're working in the free-enterprise system, whether you're running your own business or working for a multinational corporation, the demands on your time will be great. So great is this demand, reports Suzanne Gordon, in an August 20, 1989, article in the *Boston Globe*, that for millions of Americans it has made the workplace a prison. But protesting, reports Gordon, is tantamount to admitting your lack of commitment to the job. The majority of her interviewees demanded anonymity for fear that disclosing these sentiments would hurt their careers.

While there is much talk about balancing work and family,

no one in corporate America is advocating less time on the job. In fact some observers of the job market suggest that opportunities for advancement are becoming increasingly available to divorced men and single women, who have less complicated lives to manage than do married people. Although technological advances like fax machines and cellular phones could result in streamlined and efficient work, leading to less demands on one's time, the opposite has occurred. It's as though someone merely speeded up the track and all the rats were forced to run faster. On a recent vacation I observed someone faxing material to a home office from a telephone at the beach!

This trend does not bode well for those job seekers wanting to preserve their discretionary time, but there are some things the discerning job seeker can do. Certain types of organizations are more demanding than others. Clearly, entrepreneurial companies are more likely to demand long hours than companies that are relatively static (an admitted rarity). While global competiton has increased demands on all sorts of companies to produce more faster, some smaller companies avoid this trap (at least for the short term). A small business with a distinct market niche may prove less demanding than companies that have competitors lining up at their customers' door.

Most observers of the U.S. workplace concede that the time crunch does seem to be a significant problem. However, in this last decade of the twentieth century, when America will be facing the greatest global competition in its history, they also concede that things are not likely to get better—at least not for a while. Although there appears to be no way to ensure that your time will be protected, it may be comforting to know you're not alone. More important, if time is really important to you, you may want to seek out organizations that respect an individual's personal time. There aren't many out there, but for those of you for whom it is really important, it might be worth the search.

QUESTIONS TO HELP YOU CHOOSE

There are many questions you can ask your interviewers to help you discover whether the company you're approaching is a good match. While you want to be careful not to ask these questions prematurely, it's important to get answers to them at some time before negotiating the position.

Questions on the Future of the Organization

Knowing what the current leaders of the organization see for that organization in the short and long term can help you decide whether the organization is a good one for you to join.

Possible Questions

Where do you see this company five years from now?
What are the company's long- and short-term goals?
What is your vision of this company down the road?
What opportunities and threats do you see facing this company in the near future?
To what extent has this company met its projected goals in the past?
What in your opinion is this company's strongest asset for ensuring a prosperous future?

Questions on the Future of the Position

Knowing what part the job you are considering plays in the future of the organization is important. Is the role crucial to the success of the organization, or is it secondary? Understanding the importance of the position can indicate your potential in that organization.

Possible Questions

Why was this position created?
In what ways does the person in this position contribute to the company?
Under what circumstances, if any, might this position be eliminated?
Where have the people who have had the position in the past gone from here?

Questions on Expectations

Companies may vary in their expectations of employees. Finding out what a prospective employer expects before accepting a position can save you from a great deal of surprise, and perhaps disappointment. While ultimately you never know what a job is like until you're in it, asking the right questions can give you a tentative view and help you make the right choices.

Possible Questions

> What would a typical day in this position be like?
> What is the basis on which you judge success in this position?
> What would be the criteria for a raise or promotion in this position?
> What are the standards for rewards, and what are the rewards?

Attitudes About Change, Growth, and Organizational Development

Some companies view themselves as fluid and ever-changing. Other organizations see themselves as stable, secure, and relatively predictable. Depending on your personal and career goals you may want an organization that sees itself as one way or the other. While most organizations today cannot avoid change, the quality of work life would be quite different in one that thrives on change versus one that is most concerned with staying the course.

Possible Questions

> What kind of growth do you see for the company in the near future?
> Who do you see as your chief competition?
> What key factors do you think will determine this company's growth?
> In what ways do you think this company and working in it will change in the near future?

POWER NEGOTIATING

The other day I spoke with a woman who had received a call for an informal luncheon interview for a position at a television station. The woman wanted to talk with me about strategies for negotiating salary and benefits. She also wanted to talk about whether or not she really wanted the job and the questions she should ask that would help her to decide.

After a few minutes of listening to all her anxieties about the upcoming meeting I suggested she slow down, relax, and forget about negotiating or whether she wanted the position. Her task for this first meeting, I told her, was to impress the interviewer. If the luncheon ended by leaving the interviewer with the desire to talk to her more, she would have accomplished a great deal.

What this woman didn't realize was that in the negotiation process, timing is everything. The task of the first interview, especially the informal interview, is to get a second interview. The time to think about whether or not you want a position is just before it's about to be offered.

A Small Window of Time

The time to negotiate terms is right after the offer has been made. We like to tell people that during the selection process there is a small window of time during which negotiation is most fruitful. It is during that period that you have the power to negotiate. That time is the period between the moment the offer is made and the moment you accept. Prior to an offer you have no power since there's been no articulation that you are wanted. Once you've accepted the offer the interviewer has gotten what he or she wants; therefore it is not necessary to negotiate. Keeping this window in mind will lead to more effective negotiation and greater likelihood of getting what you want.

Preparation for Negotiation

The best way to ruin the negotiation process is not to prepare for it. Many people, caught up in the excitement of the prospect of a new job, assume that they can effectively negotiate without preparation. They are making a serious mistake that could very well cost them thousands of dollars a year. Unless you are clear about what your own needs are and the potential for the position, you are at a distinct disadvantage in the negotiation process. Many people say that they can determine their own needs, but finding out the potential for a position is difficult. They are mistakenly operating under the assumption that potential salaries are well-guarded secrets.

We know a man who was head of anaesthesiology in an area hospital, earning $48,000 a year. He applied for a job in a similar hospital in a nearby state. He got the job and accepted the offer of $55,000 a year. He was thrilled with his victory until he discovered that the posted range for the position was $52,000 to $62,000 a year. His perspective dramatically changed from happiness over a $7,000 gain to disappointment at having accepted a salary at the low end of the range. In his case, a simple phone call to personnel would have given him the range and provided an opportunity to procure an additional $7,000 yearly, thus doubling his increase. When seeking salary information, the first thing to do is to contact the prospective employer's personnel department to see if the figure is posted. You'll often get a range. If they say the salary range is unavailable your problem is a little more complicated, but not much. The next step involves just a little creativity. If you know someone in that organization you may have access to the salary information you need (it's amazing how closely people pay attention to these things). If you have no contacts in your prospective organization and no way you can think of for finding out the salary range, you may need to do a bit of daring investigative work.

Identify a company that is comparable to the one you're approaching in as many ways as possible. Track down someone in that organization who does similar work to the type you're applying for. Tell that person your situation and ask if he or she would mind telling you his or her salary, or at least what a reasonable salary would be for someone starting out in that position. You'll find that most people have been in your dilemma and will gladly share the information with you. All you need to do is ask!

Breaking the Price Ice

If at all possible you should wait for the interviewer to bring up the salary question. If you bring it up prematurely you may run the risk of appearing unseemly. You also put yourself in the position of having to name a figure before you've really had a chance to sell yourself.

Once the interviewer broaches the topic you must decide whether you are ready to negotiate. As mentioned earlier, the negotiating is best left to the time after an offer has been made. If the offer has been made and you feel you have had enough time to represent yourself, enter into the negotiation. If the offer has not been clearly made (these things are sometimes unclear) you may respond to the interviewer by asking, ''Does this mean you are offering me the job?'' If the interviewer says yes, proceed with the negotiation. If the response is no, say something to the effect of ''I'm sure we can work something out, but I'd prefer to negotiate once you're prepared to make an offer.'' This may at first startle the interviewer, but he or she will quickly recognize and respect your need and ability to negotiate from a position of strength. If not, the company is probably not worth working for.

Stacking Your Deck

If you're worth top dollar, and we're assuming you are, one of the ways to get it is to arm yourself for negotiation. The way to arm yourself is to identify those things about you as an applicant that separate you from the rest of the pool. We recently spoke with a woman who applied for a job in her current organization that was a step up. She was startled during negotiation to be offered $500 more a year than she was presently earning. What's more, she knew that the man currently in the position was earning $12,000 more than she was offered (a common problem for women in the marketplace). She asked for a day to consider the offer (a reasonable request), went home, and drew up a list of why she was uniquely qualified for the job and deserved more money. She went in the next day with the list and, by the end of the negotiation, received an offer within $500 of her predecessor's salary.

While not every case will have as happy an ending, particularly if you're dealing with discriminatory practices, what's important here is the action the woman took. If you're after top dollar, most interviewers want to be persuaded that you're worth it. The best approach is to enter negotiation with a solid rationale for your high salary. A mediocre approach will lead to a mediocre salary. A powerful approach will lead to a formidable salary.

Don't Take It Personally

Since you're talking about your livelihood when negotiating salary it's easy to get emotional. As soon as you do, you've lost significant ground. It's important to remember that in the best case the negotiation is not a battle but a meeting of the minds. While you have certain needs and salary requirements, the person you're dealing with also has a set of requirements and other people to whom he or she is accountable.

This is not a contest to see who can make the better deal. It's an attempt to come to an agreement on a fee for services. This is difficult to remember since the process by design implies a long-term relationship. While your goal is to get top dollar, your method should be a rational presentation of why you're worth it, not an emotional plea for why you want it.

The biggest problem with a personal plea is that it creates an imbalance of power. If the interviewer perceives a sense of weakness in you, he or she may take advantage of your vunerability. If on the other hand you project a sense of arrogance, you will trigger the other's need to control the situation and you will soon have a battle of egos, a real lose-lose situation.

Although it's true that you probably have more to lose than the interviewer does, it's important to remember that the other party is under pressure as well. A successful recruiter, or anyone with hiring responsibility, must develop a successful track record for choosing and procuring good people. If you've made it this far, the company is invested in getting you. Don't ruin the opportunity by creating a power struggle.

A Joint Venture

When there's something that you really want but are not sure you're going to get, it's hard to see that you are engaged in a cooperative process. At its best the interviewing process is a cooperative venture, the outcome of which will be a joint decision that leaves both parties satisfied. When you think about it, this makes a lot of sense. The ultimate goal for both parties is to create a good match between an individual and a job. The best way to do so is to see and approach the interviewer as an ally, not an opponent. By entering into the relationship with the goal of exploring the possibilities of a potential match, you create conditions that are likely to lead to a successful outcome.

POWER PREP STRATEGY VI

This chapter focused on gaining a clearer sense of the kinds of environments most appropriate for you to pursue given your current needs and interests. By completing this Power Prep Strategy you will have a better idea of which types of interviews to pursue and how to indicate that you are a good match.

What types of products and/or services really excite you? _____

_____

_____

What size organization do you want to work in? Why? _____

_____

What general hours do you want to work? What hours are you willing to work? _____

_____

How much money do you want to earn? What is the minimum you are willing to accept? _____

_____

What divisions or departments of an organization most interest you?

_____

This chapter talked about four primary focus points for a person's work (pages 200–201). Of these four, what percentage would you like to focus on each? What are your reasons? (Your total should equal 100 percent.)

Mastery   _____ %   reason _____

Exploration _____ % reason _____

Protection _____ % reason _____

Caretaking _____ % reason _____

This chapter discussed four different types of organizations in the free-enterprise system that you might want to work in. Decide how much of your time you want to spend interviewing in each of the types of organizations and state why. For clarification on the four types see pages 203–206. (Once again your total should equal 100 percent.)

The Fortune 500 _____ % reason _____

Up and coming companies _____ % reason _____

Support industries _____ % reason _____

Small business _____ % reason _____

In this chapter you were presented with 18 questions that you might ask from four different categories. While you will be expected to ask questions that address your needs as well as those of the organization, it is unlikely that you will have the opportunity to ask all 18 questions. Choose one question to ask from each of the four categories that most addresses your particular needs in this interview.

Question on the future of the organization

_____

_____

Question on the future of the position

_____

_____

Question on expectations

_____

_____

Question on attitudes about change, growth, and organizational development

_____

_____

Epilogue

By reading *Power Interviews* and completing the six Power Prep Strategies you have prepared yourself for making every interview a winning interview. Careful reading of this book and thorough completion of all the activities in it will enable you to deliver a high-performing interview every time. The following is a summary of the key areas you should have mastered.

- Fine-tune the basics of personal presentation.
- Use the inside secrets of interviewing.
- Research the employer.
- Identify and control your personal stressors.
- Understand the needs of the interviewer.
- Demonstrate your mastery of the seven key evaluation factors.
- Refine your answers to the 50 most commonly asked questions.
- Understand and use the key business trends for the 1990s.
- Master your ability to connect with the interviewer.
- Choose a work style that matches your needs.
- Formulate questions to ask in an interview.
- Refine your negotiation skills.

Use the preceding points as a checklist for your interview preparation. Once you have covered each of the key points thoroughly you are as prepared as you can be for power interviewing. Go out there, get the interviews, and watch the offers come pouring in!

Index

Dr. Neil Yeager presents lectures and seminars and consults in a variety of areas, including career management, organizational development, risk taking, managing change, mentoring, and leadership. For more information, call or write

Neil Yeager
P.O. Box 592
N. Amherst, MA 01059
(413) 545-1957

Lee Hough is CEO of the Xsell team, which produces and markets a range of video and software products on career development and small business management. For information on the Xsell Team's product line contact

The Xsell Team
6617 N. Scottsdale Rd.
Suite 101
Scottsdale, AZ 85253
1-800 426-8804